The
SOUTHERN
CAST IRON
COOKBOOK

The SOUTHERN CAST IRON COOKBOOK

Comforting Family Recipes to Enjoy and Share

ELENA ROSEMOND-HOERR

Photography by Cameron Whitman Photography, LLC
Food Styling by Danielle Esposti

ROCKRIDGE PRESS

For general information on our other products and services or to obtain technical support, please contact our Customer Care Department within the United States at (866) 744-2665, or outside the United States at (510) 253-0500.

Rockridge Press publishes its books in a variety of electronic and print formats. Some content that appears in print may not be available in electronic books, and vice versa.

Photography © 2017 Cameron Whitman Photography, LLC/Stocksy
Food Styling by Danielle Esposti
Pages 10 & 15: S. Lamb Photography
Author photo © Elena Rosemond-Hoerr

ISBN: Print 978-1-939754-08-0 | eBook 978-1-62315-889-7

To my father, whose love of cast iron inspired mine,
and who taught me that there is only
one way to properly fry an egg.

CONTENTS

INTRODUCTION

FOR AS LONG AS I CAN REMEMBER, there has always been a cast iron skillet on my stove. In fact, my father's most prized possession—right up there with his boat—is his cast iron skillet. I was raised with the understanding that a good cast iron skillet can cook nearly anything, from caramel sauce to corn bread. Over the years, I've put that theory to the test, cooking almost every meal in a 12-inch skillet I found in my friend's yard and carefully restored. That's the beauty of cast iron, and what has ultimately made it a staple in Southern kitchens for generations—it lasts. Treat it well, keep it seasoned, and it can be passed from grandparents to grandchildren and beyond.

Growing up in North Carolina's Piedmont region, I always knew that food was at the heart of my family's culture. Food is what brings us together, and cooking and sharing food has always been how we express love. I logged hours sitting on a stool in my grandmother's kitchen, pouring my heart out to her as she pan-roasted pork chops or kneaded dough to make dinner rolls. These days I relish the role of host, vying for the opportunity to have my family and friends over for meals both big and small. Nothing fills my heart with joy quite as much as standing in my kitchen, cooking and chatting with the people who mean the most to me.

The author's grandmother, Barbara Rosemond, in her kitchen in Chapel Hill, North Carolina.

One of the most precious pieces of cast iron in our family is my great-grandmother's cast iron cauldron. Originally a laundry pot, this 40-quart cauldron has been used for the past

100 years to make Brunswick stew each winter, a process that takes almost a week and completely consumes the maker. This cauldron, along with the cast iron skillet and griddle I inherited from my grandmother, were the beginning of my cast iron collection, and I've eagerly added pieces over the years. I have that first 12-inch skillet I restored (which never leaves my stove top), a griddle, a biscuit pan, a grill pan, a Dutch oven (for camping), and an enameled Dutch oven. I also have an 8-inch pan that I accidentally set on fire last year (pregnancy brain) awaiting restoration.

In writing this book, I've taken a hard look at the cast iron I rely on most, and have written recipes to complement these skillets and pans. Every piece serves a function in my family's daily life, and I've created the recipes to bring out the best in each. For everyday use, one-skillet meals, baking, frying, and pan roasting, my 8-inch, 10-inch, and 12-inch skillets are key. When it comes to pancakes, pizza, steak, and more, I rely on my griddle (with a grill side!). For biscuits, pies, and individually cooked and portioned dishes, I love my biscuit pan. And for soups, stews, braised meats, roasts, and breads, I couldn't live without my enameled cast iron Dutch oven.

Throughout this book, you'll see why these pieces have become the foundation of my cookware.

The author, age 4. Her start in the kitchen began with the important role of "brownie batter tester."

When I graduated from college in 2008, I started a blog, *Biscuits and Such*, because I was homesick for the people and the food I'd left behind. I wanted a place where I could experiment as a Southerner in the kitchen, bringing together family recipes and food inspired by the Southern food culture I cherish. For the past eight years, I've been working toward that goal, revisiting classic family and Southern dishes, such as Dutch Oven Brunswick Stew (page 136) and the Blueberry Mountain Pie (page 163) my grandma made for my birthday every year, and coming up with my own new favorites, like Goat's Milk and Pimento Cheese Squash Blossoms (page 76)—fried squash blossoms filled with pimento cheese and dipped in a goat milk batter. This book is an outgrowth of my years-long (if not lifelong) culinary passion: A collection of recipes that shows you the best of our family's recipes, along with a few new dishes that highlight what is wonderful about Southern food and cast iron cooking.

Welcome to the Cast Iron World! I know you're going to love it.

CHAPTER ONE

CAST IRON LOVE

In addition to the 12-inch cast iron skillet that lives on my stove top lying in wait, ready to fry an egg or sauté a handful of greens, my impeccably-cared-for collection resides in the cupboard above the stove. My 12-inch skillet gets called to duty at least twice a day to cook for our family. It moves seamlessly from frying bacon to making caramel sauce, asking only that we clean it gently and season it regularly. This skillet is my pride and joy—one I imagine will be with me for as long as I am able to fry myself a morning egg.

Still Cooking

In addition to my beloved 12-inch skillet, I have a number of other cast iron pieces—some I acquired new, some I've salvaged and restored myself, and some that were passed down from my grandmother and great-grandmother. One reason cast iron is so beloved is that when treated well, it can easily outlast its owners. My family's prized cast iron possession is my great-grandmother Sybil's cauldron, a 40-quart behemoth used annually to make Cauldron Brunswick Stew (page 138). This cauldron was originally a laundry pot, the type common among early European settlers throughout the colonies. We're not sure how long Sybil's cauldron has been in the family, but since we have deep roots in the foothills and mountains of North Carolina, I like to imagine it has traveled through the generations, evolving from a utilitarian laundry pot to a beloved heirloom fixture that helps connect us to the food culture and history of our state.

When I talk about this book with people who don't regularly cook with cast iron, many ask whether the focus is on cooking over an open flame and camping. While this book is primarily dedicated to using cast iron cookery every day in your home, it's true that cast iron performs beautifully over a campfire. That is one of the things that made it a staple for colonists and pioneers—it can withstand high temperatures and still cook food evenly and consistently. Camping was a favorite family pastime when I was growing up, and nothing beats the feeling of waking up to the chill of the morning, breathing life into the coals, and frying up a skillet full of bacon and eggs.

One reason I am able to make Brunswick stew in Sybil's cauldron, or cook a steak on my grandmother's grill pan, is that cast iron is made out of simple, sturdy material and is built to last. Unlike glazed and coated aluminum pans, cast iron is chemical free and actually adds iron to the food you cook in it (a big selling point for someone who, like me, struggles with anemia). It is also incredibly adaptable, which means that the same skillet can go from campfire to stove top to oven, making everything from a perfect Skillet Fried Eggs (page 27) to a sizzling Pan-Seared Steak (page 146) to Chocolate Chip & Walnut Banana Bread (page 43).

Buying New Cast Iron Cookware

My favorite gift to give when friends and family get married is a new 10-inch cast iron skillet, with a note that says, "When treated well, a marriage and a cast iron skillet will both last a lifetime." When buying a new skillet, I look for preseasoned ones that are thick with a heavy bottom. I choose preseasoned because, even though the amount of seasoning done before it's sold is minimal, it's a helpful jump-start. Cast iron, like good-quality leather and your favorite pair of jeans, only gets better with time. The more it's used, the better the seasoning, and the more efficiently it cooks.

A 10-inch skillet is my favorite cast iron piece to give because it's a manageable starter size. That said, a quick survey of my friends and family shows the 12-inch size is very popular for people who rely heavily on their cast iron. If you're investing in one piece, I recommend a 12-inch skillet as a solid choice that will allow you to fry, roast, sear, and bake easily.

Vintage Cast Iron

My beloved 12-inch skillet? (Yes, the one I found abandoned in a friend's backyard.) Well, I spent every evening for a few weeks carefully restoring it (see page 19) while watching episodes of *Criminal Minds,* a process I shared on my blog. Following my father's instructions step by step, I transformed the piece from very damaged and pretty gross to beautifully gleaming and ready for work.

When you're scouring flea markets, thrift shops, and yard sales, try to imagine the bones of the cast iron and what it can be when fully restored, as well as the amount of time you're willing to commit to restoring it. Not everyone has endless hours of crime fighting to watch or the time to sit and sand layers of rust and debris off a pan. (I certainly don't these days with a new baby!) So don't pick up a piece that looks like it survived the Civil War if you don't have the availability to bring it back to its former glory. But if it has a small amount of rust, scaling, or simply looks like it has seen better days, it's probably worth buying and giving it a quick seasoning (see page 17) at home.

GOOD VINTAGE OR BAD VINTAGE

Generally speaking, the cast iron cookware you find at yard sales and flea markets can usually be salvaged if you have the time and energy to put into it. Rust, scaling, and debris are all relatively easy to combat with coarse sea salt, a wire brush, elbow grease, and determination. There are, however, some types of damage that are difficult, if not impossible, to fix outside the foundry. Cast iron that is warped, severely cracked, or pitted from erosion is beyond repair by the casual consumer and should be avoided.

Foundry Logos and Markings

Collectors and aficionados of cast iron are familiar with the various foundry markings and logos found on the bottom of cast iron pieces and the inherent value these convey. On the bottom of vintage cast iron you will often find these types of markings:

- **Logos and brands:** A logo on the bottom of a cast iron skillet marks it as a product of the particular foundry where it was made. While there were many brands making cast iron in the United States and Canada during the late eighteenth and early nineteenth centuries, the most common were Griswold, Wagner, and Lodge.

  Griswold was in business from 1865 to 1957. Based out of Erie, Pennsylvania, Griswold began to manufacture skillets and other cast iron cookware in 1870. Their cast iron has a reputation for quality and durability, and their pieces are now collector's items.

  Wagner Manufacturing Company was founded in Sidney, Ohio, in 1881, and was open until 1999. They began manufacturing cast iron cookware in 1891, and made it a core part of their company's mission to make good-quality products that could live up to the name stamped on the bottom.

Lodge Manufacturing was founded in 1896 in South Pittsburg, Tennessee, and is one of America's oldest cookware manufacturers still in continuous operation. Much of the new cast iron available on the market today is made by Lodge, and the company is still owned by descendants of the founder, Joseph Lodge.

- **Numbers and letters:** At first glance it's easy to assume the number stamped on the bottom of your skillet is the size of the skillet, but it's actually a completely different size indicator. When wood-burning stoves were commonly used in people's homes, it was important to use cookware that fit the "stove eye," the opening in the top of the stove. Brands such as Wagner made skillets to fit the various-sized options for wood-burning stove eyes, which often continued as standard sizes even after gas and electric stoves became more popular. (This is why you see cast iron available in quarter sizes, such as 10¼ inches.) These dimensions were not common among brands, so a #3 Wagner may be a different size than a #3 Griswold.

- A number followed by a letter is called a "pattern letter." Foundries used different patterns of popular cast iron sizes so they could maximize production output. Each pattern was noted with a letter, so if there were problems, it could easily be traced back to the source and controlled.

- As cast iron popularity and demand increased, the numbers on the bottom of a piece evolved and often became longer. These longer numbers are not size indicators, but rather catalog numbers which are unique to the manufacturer and generally correlate with earlier dimension and pattern numbers.

- **Buying tips:** The first thing to consider when buying cast iron is what you have space and time for, and whether it needs restoration. It isn't necessarily a great investment of time or space to buy every piece that comes your way. When collecting pieces, you can choose based on brand, pan type, or characteristics of individual pieces. If your goal is to collect as many unique pieces of Griswold as you can find, stick with that strategy and get hunting. If you primarily use your cast iron for one type of cooking, such as roasting, keep your eyes peeled for pieces that will help you in that venture. Shopping based on need, collecting goals, and budget is the strategy that seems to work best for the fledgling cast iron enthusiast.

It's also important to consider which pieces you want to add to your collection. If you're willing and able to invest two to three hours on a rusted 10-inch skillet, it's worth it. However, new cast iron cookware is easily available and affordable, so a store purchase may be a better choice. If you happen upon a unique, unusual, or heirloom piece that would be hard to come by new or in good condition, snatch it up and put some elbow grease into it!

Because of cast iron's longevity, it is often passed from generation to generation. You may find yourself in this position, having inherited a few of your grandmother's pieces. If you're not sure where to start, I recommend a base-level cleaning (scrubbing with hot water and a coarse bristle brush) and reseasoning (see page 18) when you acquire it. These first steps also apply to both new pieces and those that come to you by way of yard sales or inheritance.

What Is Seasoning?

When people talk about cast iron, both old and new, they often talk about "seasoning" it. I've learned that this term gives cast iron an air of mystery and can unfortunately scare people from using it. "Seasoning" is a layer of fat that has polymerized and bonded with the iron. This seasoning protects the iron and gives it a beautiful shine and luster. It is something that you can build up over time, but it can also be damaged. As such, cast iron owners will often talk of "reseasoning" and maintenance—two things that are central to working with cast iron. The benefit of seasoned cast iron is that it has a smooth, well-oiled surface that is durable and naturally nonstick. Once an ideal level of seasoning has been achieved, it is easy to maintain through regular care and cleaning. Occasionally, you may find you need to reseason your cookware, which is usually as simple as cleaning and reoiling it a few times to restore it to its formerly pristine state. Well-seasoned cast iron will be pitch black with a natural, slick patina and a soft shine that invites you to put it to work.

CAST IRON DOS AND DON'TS

Do:

- Clean it immediately after use, every time.

- Dry it completely after use, every time.

- Keep it oiled.

- Treat it with care.

Don't:

- Use harsh or abrasive cleaners. Cast iron is porous, so I don't put anything in my skillet that I wouldn't want on my eggs.

- Soak in water for more than 20 minutes

- Leave it wet to air-dry on its own—this leads to rust spots

- Scrape at it. I do use metal spatulas, but take care not to dig into the seasoning.

- Put it in the dishwasher

Seasoning New Cookware

You'll have more success with cast iron if you take the time to season it well. The following instructions work for those sold as "preseasoned" or "unseasoned." (Even preseasoned pans benefit from additional seasoning before use.)

1. Scrub the cookware: Pour in ½ cup coarse sea salt and give it a good scrub with a towel. This will take care of any grime it has picked up on its journey from the factory to your home.

2. Wash it with soap and hot water.

3. Place it on the stove over medium heat until it is completely dry.

4. Oil the cookware (warm from the stovetop) with vegetable oil, such as olive, coconut, or peanut. Start with about 1 tablespoon for a 12-inch skillet, using more as needed to coat it thoroughly on all sides. Drain off any excess.

5. Preheat the oven to 450°F. Place the cast iron in the oven for 30 minutes. Turn off the oven and let it cool completely in the oven. Repeat this process of oiling and baking three or four times until it is pitch black and slick.

FROM BARNACLED BOAT TO SEASONED BEAUTY

I chronicled the restoration of my found 12-inch pan, step by step, in a series for my blog *Biscuits and Such*. Over the course of the series, I got more than one email from my father giving me feedback and tips. He had recently taken on the project of restoring his grandmother Sybil's cauldron, a process that started with an electric sander and finished with him burning "the bejesus out of it." Much of the work of restoration is removing layers of debris and rust, and stripping the pan all the way to bare iron before building the seasoning back up. In the case of a large or especially damaged piece, such as Sybil's cauldron (which had been sitting outside for a few years), an electric sander is just the tool to cover a lot of ground quickly. A smaller project, such as my skillet, was managed with steel wool, sandpaper, and motivation.

Once the cast iron has been stripped of all rust and debris, both my father and the good people at Lodge recommend *lighting it on fire*. When I posted about this step in my "Cast Iron Chronicles" series, I immediately got a *very* strongly worded email from my father

exclaiming that I'd used too much oil. He was right. I had taken the recommendation from the Lodge website—to use a "thin layer"—too far, and had very narrowly avoided setting our small Baltimore back patio on fire. Luckily, my Eagle Scout husband had insisted on having a fire extinguisher ready, just in case.

The *proper* approach to oiling a pan is to coat a paper towel or dishrag (my preference) with oil and rub down the pan, draining off excess oil so there is none pooling in it, and expose it to high heat over an open flame. (We generally accomplish this with a propane burner outside, but a grill is also a good option.) Bringing it past its smoke point releases the toxins built up in the pan and helps restore the iron. I recommend having baking soda on hand to extinguish any fire that does start in your pan. Once the pan cools completely, give it a quick scrub with steel wool and sandpaper, and wash it with hot, soapy water. Rinse it until the rag wipes clean, then proceed with the seasoning instructions as though it were a new pan (see page 17).

Reseasoning Cookware

You may find your cast iron occasionally needs a quick reseasoning. Anytime you notice a chink in the seasoning, a spot of rust, or a dry spot that returns even after the pan has been oiled, it's a good idea to reseason.

Reseasoning is much the same as seasoning a new pan, with the addition of first removing the damage. Depending on how damaged it is, you may want to scour it with steel wool, sandpaper, or (in dire circumstances) an electric sander. My father swears by the third method, but since I like to watch crime dramas while I restore my cast iron, I usually stick to the two-step approach of steel wool followed by sandpaper. Once all the rust has been worked out of the pan, proceed with the seasoning steps for a new pan, starting with the sea salt scrub (see page 17).

Care and Maintenance

Like every subject on the Internet, you can find arguments for and against every method of caring for cast iron, so I'll lay out the methods I was taught by my father and grandmother, and what has (and hasn't) worked for me. My great-uncle Everett recalls that his mother, Sybil, only used salt to clean her cast iron, never water, and my father falls strictly in the "never soap" school of maintenance. Here are my step-by-step instructions for cleaning cast iron after cooking:

1. Immediately after cooking, rinse your cast iron. If what you've been working with is particularly messy or stuck to the surface, it is absolutely fine to soak it for 20 minutes. Try not to leave water sitting in your cast iron longer than this. You can also loosen firmly attached food by filling it with water and bringing to a boil.

2. Use a rag or coarse brush to scrape out any food or grease and rinse it with hot water until completely clean on both the top and bottom. I avoid soap, though an occasional small amount will not hurt the cast iron.

3. Put the wet cast iron piece on the stove top over low heat until it dries completely.

4. Coat it with vegetable oil before storing it.

MAKE THE MOST OF YOUR CAST IRON

While it's probably no surprise that your cast iron skillet is the perfect tool for searing a steak or cooking a batch of pancakes, there are some ways to use your cast iron that will surprise you. Here are some tips to help you get the most use out of your cast iron.

- **Make panini:** Use two skillets (10-inch and 12-inch). Preheat both skillets and butter the bread on both sides. Place the sandwich in the larger skillet and place the smaller skillet (make sure the bottom is clean and well seasoned) on top. Cook for 3 to 4 minutes total, flipping the panini once at the halfway point.

- **Bake:** Use your skillet as a pie dish or baking pan for all manner of baked goods, from cinnamon rolls to Irish soda bread.

- **Serve:** Take it from stove top to oven to table. Cast iron is able to move seamlessly from burner to broiler. And, when you're ready to eat, put down a trivet and serve dinner straight from your skillet.

- **Go camping:** Cast iron is fantastic for use at the campground. Place it directly in the coals or on a rack over an open flame to cook three meals (and dessert!) at your campsite.

- **Grill:** Cast iron also works well on a grill, making it an essential part of big holiday meals or dinner parties, when all burners and the oven are occupied.

- **Satisfy pizza cravings:** Use your cast iron skillet to make easy Griddle Pizzas (page 46), or use it as a pizza stone by turning it upside-down, heating it in the oven, and placing your pizza directly on the overturned bottom.

- **Get creative:** Cast iron skillets are heavy as sin, so they come in handy when you need a weight in the kitchen. Use yours to crush graham crackers for pie dough, flatten a piece of meat, or press out your freshly made farm cheese.

Cooking with Cast Iron

Cast iron is truly versatile and ideal for cooking many types of foods. My husband Dan likes to tell the story of the time I used our skillet on Saturday night to make Caramel Sauce (page 158), and the next morning used the same skillet (after cleaning it, of course) to cook bacon. The bacon had just the slightest essence of caramel, and it was divine. Cast iron really shines for dishes that move from stove top to oven, because it gets hot and maintains the desired heat level perfectly. Nothing fries an egg like a well-seasoned cast iron skillet, and the same skillet can turn around and create crispy Buttermilk Fried Chicken (page 114) or humble Hush Puppies (page 82). Cast iron can also be a lovely tool for baked goods, from Skillet Corn Bread (page 50) to Cinnamon Streusel Coffee Cake (page 60).

There are foods, however, that I avoid cooking in cast iron, though that list is quite short. Scrambled eggs, for one, are not my favorite to cook in cast iron because of the amount of sticking and scraping inherent in the dish. In addition, newly seasoned cast iron doesn't handle acidity well. So until it has a nice layer of fat on it, avoid dishes with tomatoes or wine that simmer for long periods of time. Finally, while cast iron is lovely for both seafood and desserts, nothing is worse than pancakes that taste like last night's mahi-mahi. I've learned from experience that it is best to have a dedicated "seafood skillet" that can absorb as much fishy essence as it wants without flavoring your donuts.

Some cooking methods are also best avoided in cast iron. These include boiling, steaming, and anything that involves a large amount of water.

Cast iron is by no means fragile, but you do need to take a certain amount of care when working with it, including using the proper cooking utensils. Many people suggest avoiding metal utensils completely, which is a fair rule if you are heavy-handed with your spatulas. I use wooden spoons and silicone spatulas, with the exception of cooking a fried egg, for which I've had the most success with a thin, light, metal spatula and a well-seasoned skillet. But take care if you choose to use metal with your cast iron—use a light touch and do not scrape or it will damage the surface seasoning.

CHAPTER 2

BREAKFAST

BAKED BERRY OATMEAL

SERVES 4 / PREP TIME: 5 MINUTES / COOK TIME: 45 MINUTES
CAST IRON: 10-INCH SKILLET

Since becoming a mother, mornings are usually the most challenging time of day for me. I'm not a morning person and despite the fact that my son gets up at an ungodly hour, it feels like a mad rush to get us all together and out the door on time. One small thing I do to make mornings easier is prepare a batch of baked oatmeal on Sunday afternoon to eat throughout the week. Baked oatmeal is a wonderful breakfast—it's sweet, filling, and endlessly adaptable. I warm a square, top it with cottage cheese, yogurt, or a scoop of fresh berries, and have breakfast ready to go. This version features blueberries and strawberries, but it would be equally delicious with apples, peaches, apricots, or any of your favorite fruits.

2 cups rolled oats
1 cup fresh blueberries
1 cup fresh strawberries, halved
½ cup chopped pecans
1 tablespoon packed brown sugar
1 teaspoon ground cinnamon

1 teaspoon baking powder
½ teaspoon sea salt
2 eggs
1½ cups whole milk
¼ cup honey
3 tablespoons salted butter, melted

1. Preheat the oven to 350°F.

2. In a large bowl, stir together the oats, blueberries, strawberries, pecans, brown sugar, cinnamon, baking powder, and sea salt.

3. In a medium bowl, whisk the eggs, milk, honey, and butter. Fold the milk mixture into the oat mixture. Spoon the batter into the skillet.

4. Bake for 40 to 45 minutes, or until crisp around the edges and cooked through. Serve hot.

SERVING TIP: Serve topped with crème fraîche or yogurt for a deliciously quick breakfast.

DUTCH BABY PANCAKE WITH STRAWBERRIES & HONEY

SERVES 2 TO 4 / PREP TIME: 20 MINUTES / COOK TIME: 20 MINUTES
CAST IRON: 10-INCH SKILLET

Dutch baby pancakes are large, skillet-size pancakes that puff up in the oven and are a treat to make, look at, and eat. Somewhere between a pancake, a crêpe, and a popover, they are eggy and light, with a soft center and crisp edges. Not unlike cornbread, the secret to making a Dutch baby is starting with a hot skillet and transferring the batter to the oven quickly. Once served, the pancake collapses on itself, ready to be topped with fresh fruit, honey, and butter.

1 cup buttermilk

3 eggs

2 tablespoons packed brown sugar

1 teaspoon vanilla extract

¼ teaspoon ground ginger

Pinch sea salt

¾ cup all-purpose flour

5 tablespoons salted butter

1 cup fresh strawberries, quartered

2 tablespoons honey, plus more
   for serving

Maple syrup, for serving (optional)

1. Preheat the oven to 425°F.

2. Adjust an oven rack to the middle position and place the skillet on it while the oven preheats.

3. In a medium bowl, whisk together the buttermilk, eggs, brown sugar, vanilla, ginger, and sea salt. Fold in the flour gently until blended. Let the batter rest for 5 minutes.

4. Remove the skillet from the oven and add the butter to melt.

5. Pour the batter into the hot skillet and immediately put the skillet back in the oven. Bake for 15 to 20 minutes, or until golden brown and the sides have risen.

6. While the pancake cooks, in a small bowl, toss the strawberries with the honey.

7. Cut the hot pancake into wedges. Top with strawberries and honey and serve. Serve with additional honey or maple syrup (if using) for dipping.

SERVING TIP: Make these pancakes throughout the year with other seasonal fruits such as peaches and figs, or preserves and jams during the winter. Some like this pancake with a squeeze of fresh lemon juice and some confectioners' sugar sprinkled on.

CHOCOLATE BUTTERMILK STOUT PANCAKES

SERVES 4 / PREP TIME: 10 MINUTES / COOK TIME: 15 MINUTES
CAST IRON: GRIDDLE OR 12-INCH SKILLET

Our family first discovered that beer could be used in pancakes a few years ago when we woke up craving pancakes but didn't have a drop of milk in the house. A quick Google search led us to a substitution that has become a breakfast staple: the beer pancake. That first morning, we switched out the milk in the recipe for a hoppy IPA, but we've since agreed that the pancakes are best when they use both beer and buttermilk. This recipe pairs stout with cocoa powder. The bitter taste of both plays against the tang of the buttermilk and the sweetness of the chocolate chunks. Serve with salted butter between the stacked pancakes and a drizzle of local honey.

2 cups all-purpose flour
3 tablespoons sugar
3 tablespoons cocoa powder
1½ teaspoons baking powder
1½ teaspoons baking soda
2 eggs

¾ cup buttermilk
¾ cup stout
4 tablespoons salted butter, melted,
    plus more for cooking and serving
½ cup semi-sweet chocolate chunks
¾ cup pure maple syrup, warmed
    (optional)

1. In a large bowl, combine the flour, sugar, cocoa powder, baking powder, and baking soda.

2. In another large bowl, whisk the eggs, buttermilk, stout, melted butter, and chocolate chunks. Fold the egg mixture into the flour mixture.

3. On the griddle over medium heat, melt 1 tablespoon of butter. Working in batches, pour ¼-cup portions of batter onto the hot griddle. Cook for 2 to 3 minutes, or until bubbles form in the center. Flip and cook for 1 to 2 minutes, until golden brown. Repeat with the remaining butter and batter. Keep the pancakes warm in the microwave or covered loosely with a clean kitchen towel.

4. Serve hot with butter and syrup, if desired.

INGREDIENT TIP: For a lighter flavor, try a pale ale or a Kolsch instead of the stout. For a standard pancake, replace the beer with ¼ cup of buttermilk.

SKILLET FRIED EGGS

SERVES 1 / PREP TIME: 3 MINUTES / COOK TIME: 5 TO 7 MINUTES
CAST IRON: SKILLET (ANY SIZE) OR GRIDDLE

My father claims to know how to make the perfect fried egg. After years of observing his technique, I'm fairly certain his success rate is due entirely to the skillet he fries the egg in and the spatula he uses for the crucial flip. With a pat of butter (about 1 tablespoon) and a well-seasoned cast iron skillet, you too are mere minutes away from the perfect fried egg. I recommend watching the egg carefully as it cooks, and using the spatula to free the edges and test the firmness of the white before attempting a flip. In my experience, a spatula with a little bit of spring in the joint is ideal for this job.

1 egg
1 tablespoon salted butter

Pinch sea salt

1. In the skillet over medium-high heat, melt the butter.

2. Crack the egg into the skillet, on the hottest part of the skillet. Sprinkle the yolk with the sea salt.

3. Watch the egg carefully.

- For an over-easy egg: When the white has cooked through, after about 4 minutes, flip the egg while the yolk is still liquid. Cook for 1 minute and serve.

- For an over-medium egg: When the rim of the yolk has cooked through, after about 5 minutes, flip the egg and cook for 1 minute before serving.

- For an over-well egg: When the yolk has almost completely cooked through, after about 6 minutes, flip the egg and cook for 1 minute and serve.

SERVING TIP: A fried egg is a delightful breakfast on its own or served on top of the Cheesy Red Potato and Garlic Scape Hash (page 31).

SPINACH, FETA & CREMINI QUICHE

SERVES 6 / PREP TIME: 25 MINUTES / INACTIVE TIME: 1 HOUR
COOK TIME: 40 MINUTES
CAST IRON: 12-INCH SKILLET

Once I learned I could make quiche in a skillet, I never looked back. Over the years, I've tweaked this recipe slightly, adding pizza dough for crust and choosing cremini mushrooms over white button. Sometimes I add sausage or bacon; sometimes I mix in goat cheese in place of the feta. Occasionally this dish ends up on the table for brunch, but usually we whip it up for dinner. Lately I've even been making it in my cast iron biscuit pan, enjoying having seven personal quiches perfect for dinner and packed lunches. This quiche is a starting place for experiments. I promise, you won't regret trying it.

FOR THE CRUST

2 tablespoons olive oil,
     plus more for the setting bowl
¾ cup warm water
1 tablespoon active dry yeast
Pinch sea salt
Pinch red pepper flakes
2 cups bread flour, plus more for
     dusting and kneading

FOR THE FILLING

1 teaspoon olive oil,
     plus more for the skillet
8 eggs
¼ cup whole milk
2 cups fresh spinach
½ cup crumbled feta cheese
2 cremini mushrooms, sliced
2 medium shallots, diced
2 garlic cloves, minced
Pinch sea salt

TO MAKE THE CRUST

1. Coat a large bowl with olive oil and set aside.

2. In another large bowl, mix the 2 tablespoons of olive oil, water, yeast, sea salt, and red pepper flakes. Let sit for 1 minute.

3. With a wooden spoon, in the olive oil mixture, stir in the flour ½ cup at a time. Mix until it forms a loose ball. Turn the dough out onto a floured work surface (or a silicone baking mat) and knead for 5 to 7 minutes, until stretchy and pliable. Transfer the dough to the oiled bowl, cover loosely with a clean kitchen towel, and let rise for 1 hour.

1. Preheat the oven to 350°F.

2. Grease the skillet with olive oil.

3. In a large bowl, whisk the eggs and milk.

4. Stir in the spinach, feta, mushrooms, shallots, garlic, and sea salt.

TO MAKE THE QUICHE

1. Press the dough into the skillet across the bottom and up the sides. Pour the filling into the crust.

2. Brush the edges of the crust with the 1 teaspoon of olive oil.

3. Bake for 40 minutes, or until the eggs are cooked through and crust is golden brown.

PREPARATION TIP: Double the batch of dough and freeze half for later!

SOURDOUGH FRENCH TOAST WITH BAKED PEARS

SERVES 4 / PREP TIME: 10 MINUTES / COOK TIME: 25 MINUTES
CAST IRON: 12-INCH SKILLET AND GRIDDLE

The beauty of French toast is that it's a delicious base for many toppings. Use your imagination and experiment! I've tried lemon curd, hazelnut spread, berries with honey, caramelized bananas, candied ginger, toasted pecans, and even ham and Gruyère cheese—all with great success.

FOR THE BAKED PEARS
2 pears, quartered and cored
4 tablespoons salted butter, cubed
1 teaspoon ground cinnamon

FOR THE FRENCH TOAST
4 eggs
½ cup whole milk

1 tablespoon sugar
1 teaspoon vanilla extract
1 teaspoon ground cinnamon
1 teaspoon ground ginger
4 tablespoons salted butter
1 loaf crusty sourdough bread,
    cut into ¾- to 1-inch slices
Honey, for serving

TO MAKE THE PEARS

1. Preheat the oven to 350°F.

2. Place the pears in the skillet, top with the butter cubes and cinnamon, and bake for 25 minutes.

TO MAKE THE FRENCH TOAST

1. In a large, shallow bowl, whisk the eggs, milk, sugar, vanilla, cinnamon, and ginger.

2. Preheat the griddle over medium-high heat. Add 1 tablespoon of butter to melt.

3. Dip a slice of the bread in the egg mixture, submerging it completely and turning it for a full coating. Place in the hot skillet. Stir the batter before dunking each slice to ensure that the spices stay evenly distributed. Repeat with the remaining slices and the remaining butter and egg mixture.

4. Cook the bread for 2 to 3 minutes per side until crisp and browned. Keep the French toast warm in the microwave or covered loosely with a clean kitchen towel.

5. Serve warm, topped with the baked pears and a drizzle of honey.

CHEESY RED POTATO & GARLIC SCAPE HASH

SERVES 4 / PREP TIME: 20 MINUTES / COOK TIME: 15 MINUTES
CAST IRON: 12-INCH SKILLET

When we lived in Baltimore, Dan and I had a small backyard garden plot that was the source of constant excitement and frustration. We tried, and often failed, to grow a great number of things. Among our more notable successes were one very enthusiastic habanero bush and a plot of garlic. Our garlic was fantastic at producing scapes, and we spent the better part of a week loaded with the spicy green shoots that emerge skyward from the bulb. So we found a new appreciation for garlic scapes, mixing them into everything from grits to potato hash.

2 tablespoons salted butter
3 garlic cloves, minced
1 white onion, chopped
Sea salt
Freshly ground black pepper

6 to 8 small red potatoes, grated
¼ pound Cheddar cheese, grated
5 to 6 garlic scapes or scallions
    (white and light green
    parts), minced

1. In the skillet over medium heat, melt the butter

2. Add the garlic and onion. Season with sea salt and black pepper. Stir to combine.

3. Stir in the potatoes to mix thoroughly. Cook for about 15 minutes, stirring every 2 to 3 minutes, until the potatoes are cooked.

4. Remove the skillet from the heat and stir in the Cheddar cheese. Adjust the seasoning as needed, and sprinkle with garlic scapes. Serve hot.

SERVING TIP: Serve topped with a Skillet Fried Eggs (page 27) and a side of bacon for a well-rounded and filling breakfast.

POTATO & ROSEMARY FRITTATA

SERVES 6 / PREP TIME: 15 MINUTES / COOK TIME: 30 MINUTES
CAST IRON: 12-INCH SKILLET

If I'm honest, my favorite way to eat eggs is fried and I don't often stray. However, this recipe is also one of my favorites because the potatoes form a bit of a crust, allowing the eggs to remain moist and fluffy. A frittata—somewhere between an omelet, a torta, and a quiche—is well suited to cooking in a cast iron skillet because the even distribution of heat in the oven cooks the eggs nicely. This recipe benefits from the ability to move seamlessly from stove top to oven.

2 tablespoons salted butter
1 large red potato, thinly sliced
1 yellow onion, chopped
2 garlic cloves, minced
6 eggs

½ cup shredded Cheddar cheese
¼ cup water
2 tablespoons fresh rosemary leaves, chopped
Pinch sea salt

1. Preheat the oven to 350°F.

2. In the skillet, melt the butter over medium heat. Add the potato, onion, and garlic, and cook for about 10 minutes, stirring occasionally, until the potato begins to soften. Spread the mixture evenly over the bottom of the skillet.

3. In a large bowl, whisk the eggs, cheese, water, rosemary, and sea salt. Pour the egg mixture over the potato mixture in the skillet. Cook for 3 to 5 minutes, or until the eggs begin to set. Transfer the skillet to the oven.

4. Bake for 12 to 15 minutes, or until lightly browned and fluffy. Slice in wedges and serve hot.

INGREDIENT TIP: Fresh rosemary really makes this dish pop, but can be replaced easily with 1 tablespoon of dried rosemary leaves.

SWEET POTATO & CHIPOTLE BOWLS

SERVES 2 / PREP TIME: 15 MINUTES / COOK TIME: 30 MINUTES
CAST IRON: 12-INCH SKILLET

Dan and I are big fans of breakfast for dinner, and this recipe is a staple. Sweet potatoes crisp up beautifully when they're cut into noodle-like shapes, and the combination of coconut oil and chipotle is a nice blend of sweet and spicy. I like to add a fried egg, grated cheese, and scallions for a fast vegetarian dinner. It's also delicious with a bit of sausage, pulled chicken, roasted Brussels sprouts, bacon, or spinach.

2 tablespoons coconut oil

3 medium sweet potatoes, sliced into thin strips

1 tablespoon ground chipotle chile pepper

½ teaspoon sea salt

1 tablespoon salted butter

2 eggs

¼ cup shredded pepper Jack cheese

¼ cup chopped scallions (white and light green parts)

1. In the skillet, heat the coconut oil over medium heat. Toss in the sweet potatoes, chipotle pepper, and sea salt. Cook for 15 to 20 minutes, stirring occasionally, or until the potatoes are cooked through. Transfer the potatoes to a medium bowl and set aside.

2. Wipe the skillet with a paper towel, place it over medium-high heat, and melt the butter in it.

3. Crack the eggs into the hottest part of the skillet and fry them to your liking (see Skillet Fried Eggs, page 27).

4. Top each serving of potatoes with a fried egg and a sprinkling of pepper Jack cheese and scallions.

PREPARATION TIP: If you have a spiralizer, this is a great recipe for sweet potato noodles. (My husband thinks these should be called sweet patoodles!)

EGGS BENEDICT WITH ZUCCHINI-POTATO FRITTERS

SERVES 4 / PREP TIME: 15 MINUTES / COOK TIME: 30 MINUTES
CAST IRON: 10-INCH SKILLET OR GRIDDLE

Poaching eggs was something I'd always found intimidating, which meant that eggs Benedict were completely outside my comfort zone. Eventually, I decided I couldn't call myself a seasoned cook if I was too afraid to poach an egg. So I read lots of techniques and tips, and buckled down to try my hand at it. Like almost everything I've ever been afraid to try, the dish was not as hard as I expected. The key is fresh eggs (like from your neighbor's chickens or the farmers' market) and a splash of vinegar in the water. Shortly after I learned how easy poaching eggs is, I read an article about making hollandaise sauce in the blender. One thing led to another and, before I knew it, eggs Benedict were a part of my regular brunch menu rotation.

8 slices thick-cut bacon

FOR THE FRITTERS
1 zucchini, grated
1 red potato, grated
1 small white onion, grated
2 garlic cloves, minced
1 egg
2 tablespoons all-purpose flour
½ teaspoon sea salt
½ teaspoon red pepper flakes
Salted butter, for cooking

FOR THE HOLLANDAISE SAUCE
3 egg yolks
1 tablespoon freshly squeezed
    lemon juice, plus more as needed
Pinch cayenne pepper, plus more
    as needed
Pinch ground chipotle chile pepper,
    plus more as needed
Pinch sea salt, plus more as needed
½ cup (1 stick) salted butter, melted

FOR THE POACHED EGGS
4 very fresh eggs
1 tablespoon white vinegar

TO MAKE THE FRITTERS

1. In the skillet over medium heat, cook the bacon for about 6 minutes, or until it is your desired crispness, and set aside. Drain off most of the bacon fat but reserve 1 tablespoon for cooking the fritters.

2. In a large bowl, stir together the zucchini, potato, onion, garlic, egg, flour, sea salt, and red pepper flakes. With your hands, press the zucchini and potato mixture into 8 fritters. Squeeze out any excess moisture so the fritters are well formed but not dripping.

3. In the skillet (no need to wipe it out) over medium heat, melt 1 tablespoon of butter. Cook the fritters for 4 to 5 minutes per side, or until crisp and browned.

TO MAKE THE HOLLANDAISE SAUCE

1. While the fritters cook, in a blender (or food processor), add the egg yolks, lemon juice, cayenne, chipotle pepper, and sea salt, and blend to combine.

2. With the blender running, slowly pour in the melted butter. Taste and adjust the lemon juice and spices to your preference. Set aside.

TO MAKE THE POACHED EGGS

1. Heat a saucepan of water over medium-high to a steady simmer. Swirl the vinegar into the water with a spoon.

2. Crack the first egg into a cup and gently tip the egg into the swirling water. Cook for 3 to 4 minutes and remove it with a slotted spoon. Transfer to a bowl of hot water to keep warm and repeat with the remaining 3 eggs.

3. To serve, place the fritters on 4 plates and top each with a poached egg, bacon, and a generous serving of hollandaise sauce.

PREPARATION TIP: To ease some of the prep, use a food processor, if available, to grate the vegetables.

INGREDIENT TIP: Substitute paprika for cayenne pepper to make a hollandaise with just as much spice but less heat.

SAUSAGE & CHEDDAR BREAKFAST CASSEROLE

SERVE 6 / PREP TIME: 15 MINUTES / COOK TIME: 1 HOUR, 15 MINUTES
CAST IRON: 12-INCH SKILLET

Spending Christmas each year with our aunt and uncle was always a sublime coming together of family, food, and holiday magic. Aunt Jill's breakfast casseroles would come out of the oven just as we finished opening presents. She made two kinds: sausage and Cheddar casserole and vegetable casserole. Sausage and Cheddar was my favorite. Something about this hot, cheesy, spicy dish is perfect for Christmas morning.

8 eggs
1½ cups whole milk
1 teaspoon dry mustard
1 teaspoon ground paprika
1 teaspoon red pepper flakes
1 teaspoon sea salt

1 tablespoon salted butter
1 pound ground sausage
1 white onion, diced
2 garlic cloves, minced
4 cups cubed bread
1 cup shredded Cheddar cheese

1. Preheat the oven to 375°F.

2. In a large bowl, whisk the eggs, milk, mustard, paprika, red pepper flakes, and sea salt.

3. In the skillet over medium heat, melt the butter.

4. Add the sausage and cook for 8 to 10 minutes, stirring frequently, until almost cooked through.

5. Stir in the onion and garlic. Sauté for 3 to 4 minutes, until the onions are tender and the sausage is fully cooked. Remove from the heat.

6. Add the bread cubes and Cheddar cheese to the skillet and toss to combine.

7. Pour the egg mixture over the top.

8. Bake for 50 to 60 minutes, or until cooked through and puffed.

PREPARATION TIP: Assemble this the night before and stick it in the oven when you wake up. If you're making the casserole ahead of time, let the sausage cool before combining it with the egg mixture.

CANDIED BACON

SERVES 4 / PREP TIME: 5 MINUTES / COOK TIME: 20 TO 30 MINUTES
CAST IRON: 12-INCH SKILLET

When I was pregnant, Dan and I took a birth class where it was heavily impressed upon him that his job for the first few months once the baby arrived was to feed me so I could focus on feeding our child. Ever the model student, he took this to heart and made it his mission to put three balanced meals (and a few snacks) in front of me every day. While the nights were long and hard those first few months, the mornings are some of my sweetest memories. I would get up with the baby, pull him into bed with me to nurse, and Dan would bring me breakfast—usually coffee, a few eggs, and bacon. The baby and I would sit and make faces at each other while I sipped my coffee and ate. Every once in a while, Dan would top the bacon with a little sugar and spice, which felt like such a treat, especially when served to me in bed. Nothing is more rewarding and more challenging than caring for a new baby, but those breakfasts in bed made all the difference. The baby's smiles helped, too.

½ cup packed dark brown sugar
1 tablespoon ground cinnamon
1 teaspoon ground ginger

1 teaspoon ground cloves
1 tablespoon salted butter
1 pound thick-cut bacon

1. In a small bowl, stir together the brown sugar, cinnamon, ginger, and cloves.

2. In the skillet over medium heat, melt the butter.

3. Dredge each piece of bacon in spiced sugar and add to the skillet. Do not overcrowd the skillet. You will have to do this in batches. Fry the bacon for 4 to 5 minutes per side until crisp. Transfer to a wire rack to drain. Repeat until all the bacon is cooked.

SERVING TIP: Add candied bacon to your Eggs Benedict with Zucchini-Potato Fritters (page 34) for a sweet and salty brunch combination!

FRIED GRITS WITH
COUNTRY HAM & RED EYE GRAVY

SERVES 4 / PREP TIME: 45 MINUTES / INACTIVE TIME: 1 HOUR
COOK TIME: 50 MINUTES
CAST IRON: 10-INCH SKILLET

In the first months of new parenthood I gladly accepted all the extra caffeine I could get my hands on. This extended past my morning latte to include cappuccino gelato for dessert and red eye gravy on my grits. Red eye gravy is quick to whip up and made from drippings, butter, and coffee, bringing a bit of richness (along with a jolt of caffeine) to everything it touches.

FOR THE GRITS
2 cups whole milk
½ cup stone-ground yellow corn grits
1 teaspoon sea salt
1 teaspoon red pepper flakes
2 tablespoons salted butter
½ cup corn flour

FOR THE HAM AND GRAVY
5 tablespoons salted butter, divided
8 slices country ham
½ cup black coffee
1 teaspoon sea salt
1 teaspoon freshly ground
    black pepper

TO MAKE THE GRITS

1. In a medium saucepan over medium heat, combine the milk, grits, sea salt, and red pepper flakes. Cook for 20 to 25 minutes, stirring frequently, until the grits thicken. Pour into a 9-by-5-inch loaf pan and chill for at least 1 hour.

2. Preheat the oven to 200°F.

3. In the skillet over medium-high heat, melt the butter.

4. Turn the chilled grits loaf over onto a cutting board and slice into 1-inch-thick pieces. Dust each slice on both sides with the corn flour.

5. Fry the grits slices for 2 to 3 minutes per side, transferring them on a plate to the warm oven when done.

1. Wipe the skillet clean with a dry paper towel, place it back over medium-high heat, and add 1 tablespoon of the butter to melt.

2. Add the ham slices and fry for 2 to 3 minutes per side, transferring them to the warm oven when done.

3. Return the skillet to medium-high heat, and add the remaining 4 tablespoons of butter to melt.

4. Stir in the coffee, sea salt, and black pepper, scraping up and incorporating any drippings or browned bits from the ham into the gravy.

5. Pile four plates high with the grits and ham, drizzle with gravy, and serve.

VARIATION TIP: Stir 1 cup of shredded pepper Jack cheese into the grits before serving.

CHAPTER 3

BISCUITS & BREAD

DROP BISCUITS

SERVES 7 / PREP TIME: 10 MINUTES / COOK TIME: 15 MINUTES
CAST IRON: BISCUIT PAN

The year I graduated college I experienced some light career ennui and a fair amount of homesickness. The logical solution was to make food that reminded me of home, a journey that inspired my Southern food blog, *Biscuits and Such*. Almost a decade later, the blog is still going strong and has brought me to amazing places and experiences (like this cookbook!). Also still going strong is my love for biscuits—a love and appreciation that has deepened and evolved over the years. These days, my favorite way to make biscuits is with a biscuit pan: a cast iron pan that features seven 3- to 4-inch wells perfect for drop biscuits, pies, individual mac 'n' cheese portions, and more. An adaptation of classic buttermilk biscuits, drop biscuits have slightly more buttermilk and dough that you simply spoon into the pan instead of kneading and folding. They're quick, easy, and thanks to the design of the pan, delightfully crisp around the edges.

4 cups all-purpose flour
2 teaspoons baking soda
2 teaspoons sea salt

1 teaspoon baking powder
1 cup (2 sticks) cold
    salted butter, cubed
2¼ cups buttermilk

1. Preheat the oven to 400°F.

2. In a large bowl, whisk the flour, baking soda, sea salt, and baking powder.

3. Add the cold butter cubes to the flour mixture. Mix together with your hands, crumbling the butter, until the texture resembles coarse cornmeal.

4. Stir in the buttermilk just until the dough is evenly moistened

5. Spoon the dough, divided evenly, into the wells of the biscuit pan.

6. Bake for 12 to 15 minutes, or until cooked through and golden brown.

SERVING TIP: Split the biscuits and fill with country ham, white Cheddar cheese, honey, and stone-ground mustard for my current favorite biscuit sandwich.

CHOCOLATE CHIP & WALNUT BANANA BREAD

SERVES 6 TO 8 / PREP TIME: 20 MINUTES / COOK TIME: 1 HOUR
CAST IRON: 10-INCH SKILLET

I have never lived in a home that didn't have at least two brown bananas in the freezer. Bananas always seem to reach their prime on the countertop, so the best option for repurposing overripe bananas is to save them in the freezer (peel them first because it's a pain to do it after) for a future batch of banana bread! With a combination of spices, chopped nuts, chocolate chips, and those bananas, this bread is dense, sweet, and nutty. Keep this recipe ready for the day when you have enough bananas stashed away in the back of the freezer.

2 eggs
½ cup sugar
3 ripe bananas, diced
1 teaspoon ground nutmeg
1 teaspoon ground cinnamon
½ cup buttermilk

½ cup honey
1 teaspoon vanilla extract
½ cup chopped walnuts
½ cup dark chocolate chips
2 cups all-purpose flour
1 tablespoon salted butter

1. Preheat the oven to 400°F.

2. In a large bowl, whisk together the eggs and sugar.

3. Fold in the bananas, nutmeg, and cinnamon.

4. Stir in the buttermilk, honey, vanilla, walnuts, and chocolate chips.

5. Mix in the flour, ½ cup at a time, until it is completely incorporated.

6. Grease the skillet with the butter, and pour the batter into it.

7. Bake for 50 to 60 minutes, or until the top is firm when gently pressed and nicely browned.

SERVING TIP: Toast slices of banana bread and serve smeared with butter. Heaven!

FIG & LEMON SPIRAL ROLLS

SERVES 8 / PREP TIME: 30 MINUTES / INACTIVE TIME: 1 HOUR
COOK TIME: 50 MINUTES
CAST IRON: 10-INCH SKILLET

My friend Lauren has two big, beautiful fig trees in her yard that produce an impressive crop of figs twice a year—mid summer and early fall. I'm always happy to be on the receiving end of fresh figs because they quickly become jam, pizza toppings, or gelato. This year, Lauren sent me home with a big jar of dried figs that became the inspiration for this recipe. The dried figs, when rehydrated and combined with lemons, create a paste that is sweet, nutty, and tart. The flavors complement each other well, and this adaptation of the classic cinnamon roll is one I'll reach for during fig season year after year.

FOR THE ROLLS
Olive oil, for the bowl
¼ cup warm water
2½ teaspoons active dry yeast
½ cup plus 1 pinch granulated
    sugar, divided
½ cup whole milk
½ cup (1 stick) salted butter
Pinch sea salt
1 egg, beaten lightly
3½ cups all-purpose flour,
    plus more for kneading

FOR THE FIG AND LEMON FILLING
1 cup dried figs
1½ cups water

⅓ cup packed light brown sugar,
    divided
1 tablespoon freshly squeezed
    lemon juice
½ cup (1 stick) salted butter,
    at room temperature
2 tablespoons fresh lemon zest
1 teaspoon ground ginger
1 teaspoon vanilla extract
1 cup chopped walnuts

FOR THE LEMON ICING
1 cup sugar
2 tablespoons freshly squeezed
    lemon juice

TO MAKE THE ROLLS

1. Coat a large bowl with olive oil and set aside.

2. In another large bowl, whisk the warm water, yeast, and the pinch of sugar until the yeast dissolves.

3. In a small saucepan over low heat, combine the milk and butter, and heat until the butter melts. Remove from the heat, and whisk into the yeast mixture.

4. Add the ½ cup of sugar, the sea salt, egg, and 1¾ cups of flour. Stir well to combine.

5. Add the remaining 1¾ cups of flour, ½ cup at a time, and stir until it forms a dough. Turn the dough out onto a floured work surface (or a silicone baking mat), adding flour as needed to keep the dough workable, and knead for 5 minutes.

6. Transfer the dough to the oiled bowl, cover loosely with a clean kitchen towel, and let rise in a warm place for 1 hour.

TO MAKE THE FIG AND LEMON FILLING

1. While the dough is rising, in a saucepan over medium heat, combine the figs, water, and 1 tablespoon of brown sugar. Simmer for 15 to 20 minutes, or until the figs soften. Remove from the heat and cool to room temperature. Transfer to a food processor (or blender).

2. Add the lemon juice and process until it forms a paste. Transfer to a medium bowl.

3. To the fig paste, add the butter, the remaining 5 tablespoons of brown sugar, lemon zest, ginger, and vanilla. Mix thoroughly and set aside.

TO FINISH THE ROLLS

1. Preheat the oven to 350°F.

2. When the dough has risen, turn it out onto a floured work surface (or a silicone baking mat) and roll it into a 12-by-16-inch rectangle about ½ inch thick.

3. Spread the fig paste evenly over the dough. Sprinkle evenly with the walnuts.

4. Starting with the long side, roll the dough onto itself to form a tight log. Cut the dough into 8 equal slices and arrange them in the skillet, cut-side up.

5. Bake for 25 to 30 minutes, or until bubbling and golden brown.

TO MAKE THE ICING

While the rolls bake, in a small bowl, whisk the confectioners' sugar and lemon juice. When the rolls come out of the oven, immediately drizzle with the icing.

PREPARATION TIP: No dried figs? No worries. In a pinch, mix softened butter with 1 cup of fig jam and 2 tablespoons of lemon zest for a quick and easy fig filling.

BUILD-YOUR-OWN GRIDDLE PIZZA

SERVES 4 / PREP TIME: 20 MINUTES / INACTIVE TIME: 1 HOUR
COOK TIME: 15 TO 30 MINUTES
CAST IRON: GRIDDLE

One of my favorite party concepts is the "build your own" spread. This works with so many different foods—biscuits, grits, personal pizzas, Bloody Marys, French toast (page 30)—and it makes feeding a lot of guests easy and fun. When we throw grilled pizza parties, I make a big batch of dough and set out a table full of toppings—everything from fresh figs to goat cheese, prosciutto, mushrooms sautéed in butter, and fresh herbs. I stand by the griddle and fry personal dough rounds ready for each person to customize to their liking. Everyone is happy, everyone is fed, the party is a success!

FOR THE DOUGH

¼ cup olive oil, plus more
   for the bowl and grilling
1½ cups warm water
2 tablespoons active dry yeast
2 teaspoons sea salt, plus more
   for grilling
5 cups bread flour, plus more
   for kneading

TOPPING OPTIONS

Fresh arugula
Prosciutto
Cooked sausage
Mozzarella cheese
Thinly sliced red potatoes
Shredded white Cheddar cheese
Chopped scallions (white
   and light green parts)
Sautéed mushrooms
Red onion
Fresh cilantro
Fresh basil
Apples
Figs

TO MAKE THE DOUGH

1. Coat a large bowl with olive oil and set aside.

2. In another large bowl, whisk the olive oil, warm water, yeast, and sea salt. Let sit for 1 minute.

3. With a wooden spoon, stir in 2½ cups of flour until combined. Add the remaining 2½ cups of flour and, with your hands, mix until it forms a ball. Turn the dough out onto a floured work surface (or a silicone baking mat), adding flour as needed to keep the dough from getting sticky, and knead for 5 minutes or until the dough is pliable, stretchy, and well formed. Transfer the dough to the oiled bowl, cover loosely with a clean kitchen towel, and let sit for 1 hour.

TO MAKE THE PIZZAS

1. Preheat your griddle over medium-high heat.

2. Divide the dough into 8 pieces. Roll each piece into a small 6-inch round. Brush one side with olive oil and sprinkle with sea salt.

3. Place the rounds on the griddle, oiled-side down, and cook for 4 to 6 minutes. Transfer to a cutting board, cooked-side down, and brush the uncooked side with olive oil and sprinkle with sea salt.

4. Arrange your toppings of choice on the rounds. Carefully return the pizzas to the griddle and cook for 4 to 6 minutes more.

INGREDIENT TIP: Have a variety of meats, cheeses, and vegetables on hand so everyone can make their ideal pizza.

BEIGNETS

MAKES 20 / PREP TIME: 15 MINUTES / INACTIVE TIME: 6 TO 12 HOURS
COOK TIME: 20 MINUTES
CAST IRON: DUTCH OVEN OR 12-INCH SKILLET

My sister Lauren lives in New Orleans. When we first visited her, eating beignets in City Park was at the top of our must-do list. The beignet, a pastry brought to the Crescent City by eighteenth-century French colonists, is the state doughnut of Louisiana and has become an important part of Creole food culture. Something about the hot square of fried dough, topped with a generous amount of confectioners' sugar, and eaten fresh feels quintessentially New Orleans. So on that visit, we devoured the hot beignets in the fading sun, drinking café aut lait and laughing as we got confectioners' sugar *everywhere*.

Olive oil, for the bowl
½ cup hot water
1 tablespoon active dry yeast
½ cup whole milk
½ cup heavy (whipping) cream
2 tablespoons salted butter, melted
¾ cup granulated sugar

2 eggs
1 teaspoon vanilla extract
1 teaspoon baking powder
5 cups all-purpose flour,
    plus more for kneading
Peanut oil or coconut oil, for frying
Confectioners' sugar, for topping

1. Coat a large bowl with olive oil and set aside.

2. In another large bowl, whisk the hot water and the yeast until the yeast dissolves.

3. In a saucepan over medium heat, combine the milk, cream, and butter, and heat until the butter melts. Pour the milk mixture into the yeast mixture.

4. Stir in the granulated sugar, eggs, vanilla, baking powder, and 2½ cups of flour. Knead the remaining 2½ cups of flour into the dough and turn it out onto a floured surface (or a silicone baking mat), adding more flour as needed to keep the dough workable. Knead for 5 to 7 minutes, until stiff. Transfer the dough to the oiled bowl, cover loosely with a clean kitchen towel, and refrigerate for 6 hours or up to overnight.

5. In the Dutch oven or skillet over high heat, heat 1 inch of peanut oil to 375°F.

6. Flour a work surface (or a silicone baking mat), and roll the dough into a 16-by-16-inch rectangle about ½ inch thick. Cut into 3-by-3-inch squares.

7. Add the dough squares to the hot oil (you may have to do this in batches), and fry each square for 2 minutes per side, or until golden brown.

8. Transfer to a wire rack to cool slightly, and sprinkle with a generous amount of confectioners' sugar. Serve warm.

SERVING TIP: For a true New Orleans beignet experience, enjoy these with a cold glass of café au lait.

SKILLET CORN BREAD

SERVES 7 / PREP TIME: 15 MINUTES / COOK TIME: 30 MINUTES
CAST IRON: BISCUIT PAN AND 10-INCH SKILLET

Cast iron skillets can be wonderful tools for baking bread, and the classic example of this is corn bread. It comes in many forms, but my favorite is unsweetened corn bread made only with coarse yellow cornmeal and baked in a screaming-hot skillet. By preheating your skillet in the warming oven, the cornbread begins to cook as soon as the batter hits the iron. This guarantees that the corn bread will have the crisp edges that set great cornbread apart from all the rest. The addition of bacon drippings won't hurt either.

½ pound thick-cut bacon, diced
2 cups coarse yellow cornmeal
1 teaspoon sea salt
1 teaspoon baking powder
1 teaspoon baking soda

1½ cups buttermilk
4 tablespoons salted butter,
  melted, plus more for serving
1 egg

1. In the skillet over medium-high heat, cook the bacon, stirring often, for about 10 minutes, until crisp. With a slotted spoon, remove the bacon from the skillet and set aside. Reserve the drippings in the skillet.

2. Preheat the oven to 400°F.

3. Adjust an oven rack to the middle position, and put the biscuit pan in the oven while it is heating.

4. In a large bowl, stir together the cornmeal, sea salt, baking powder, baking soda, and cooked bacon.

5. In a small bowl, whisk 2 tablespoons of the reserved bacon drippings, the buttermilk, 2 tablespoons of butter, and the egg until well combined. Fold the bacon drippings mixture into the cornmeal mixture.

6. Remove the biscuit pan from the oven and brush each well with the remaining bacon drippings. Divide the batter evenly among the wells and return the pan to the oven.

7. Bake for 20 minutes, or until cooked through and browned on top.

8. Top each mini corn bread with the remaining melted butter, and serve warm.

INGREDIENT TIP: Add ¼ cup of crushed cracklin' (a piece of pork fat with the skin attached) to create a variation called "cracklin' cornbread."

PREPARATION TIP: This recipe can also be made in a 10-inch skillet. Reduce the cooking time to 12 to 15 minutes.

ROSEMARY & GARLIC DINNER ROLLS

MAKES 10 / PREP TIME: 30 MINUTES / INACTIVE TIME: 2 HOURS
COOK TIME: 35 MINUTES
CAST IRON: 12-INCH SKILLET

I had the good fortune of inheriting my grandmother's recipe cards, a collection that contains some gems (like these dinner rolls) and some that should be lost to time (a lot of gelatin). Written in her elegant cursive, they are a little vague on instructions, recommending that things be "cooked until done" in a "warm oven." Idiosyncrasies aside, these heirloom dinner rolls are a holiday staple. All nestled together in your skillet, they bake beautifully, fully realizing the dream combination of buttered crust and soft, pillowy dough. Our family loves these rolls smeared with butter or used to make sandwiches with leftover roast.

Olive oil, for the bowl
1 cup whole milk
2 tablespoons sugar
2 tablespoons shortening
1 teaspoon sea salt
¼ cup warm water
1 tablespoon active dry yeast

1 egg, beaten
2 cups bread flour, plus more
    for kneading
4 tablespoons salted butter,
    plus more for the skillet
2 garlic cloves, minced
1 tablespoon fresh rosemary
    leaves, minced

1. Coat a large bowl with olive oil and set aside.

2. In a medium saucepan over medium-high heat, scald the milk by bringing it almost to a boil and then remove it from the heat. Stir in the sugar, shortening, and sea salt, stir until the sugar and shortening melt, and let cool until lukewarm.

3. In a small bowl or cup, whisk the warm water and yeast until the yeast dissolves. Stir the yeast into the milk mixture.

4. Add the beaten egg and stir to combine.

5. Stir the flour into the yeast-milk mixture, ½ cup at a time, until it forms a soft dough. Turn the dough out onto a floured surface (or a silicone baking mat), adding more flour as necessary to prevent it from getting tacky, and knead for 10 minutes. Transfer the dough to the oiled bowl, cover loosely with a clean kitchen towel, and let rise for 1 hour.

6. Grease the skillet with butter.

7. Divide the dough into 10 pieces. Form each piece into a ball by pinching the dough at the base so the top is tight. Cluster the balls together in the skillet, pinched-side down. Cover loosely with a clean kitchen towel and let rise for 1 hour.

8. Preheat the oven to 350°F.

9. In a small saucepan over medium-low heat, melt the butter. Add the garlic and rosemary, and simmer until the garlic softens.

10. Brush the top of each roll with a generous amount of garlic butter.

11. Bake for 30 to 35 minutes, or until cooked through and golden brown. Serve hot.

PREPARATION TIP: For an extra-buttery roll, brush a second time with butter, garlic, and rosemary after they come out of the oven.

MONKEY BREAD

SERVES 4 TO 6 / PREP TIME: 20 MINUTES / INACTIVE TIME: 2 HOURS
COOK TIME: 55 MINUTES
CAST IRON: DUTCH OVEN

Growing up, we lived near my mom's Aunt Donna and Uncle Bill, whose beautiful backyard—complete with big, live oak trees and a pool perfect for parties—overlooked the Intracoastal Waterway. I spent a lot of time at their house, reading Aunt Donna's collection of Nancy Drew books and counting the wrinkles that years of laughter had left on her face (that one is going to come back to get me). Our favorite way to pass the afternoon together was to make monkey bread, rolling out the dough, dipping each ball in sugar and cinnamon, and sitting on the back patio enjoying our treat. Monkey bread, in all of its warm, gooey, sweet, caramel glory, is a food that will always remind me of home, family, and comfort.

FOR THE SUGAR COATING

1 cup packed dark brown sugar

2 teaspoons ground cinnamon

½ cup (1 stick) salted butter, melted

FOR THE DOUGH

Olive oil, for the bowl

1 cup whole milk

2 tablespoons granulated sugar

2 tablespoons shortening

1 teaspoon sea salt

¼ cup warm water

1 tablespoon active dry yeast

1 egg, beaten

2 ½ cups bread flour,
plus more for kneading

FOR THE GLAZE

4 tablespoons salted butter

½ cup packed dark brown sugar

¼ cup honey

1 tablespoon water

1 teaspoon ground cinnamon

1 teaspoon ground ginger

TO MAKE THE SUGAR COATING

In a small bowl, mix the dark brown sugar, cinnamon, and melted butter, and set aside.

1. Coat a large bowl with olive oil and set aside.

2. In a medium saucepan over medium-high heat, scald the milk by bringing it almost to a boil and then remove it from the heat. Stir in the granulated sugar, shortening, and sea salt, stir until the sugar and shortening melt, and let cool until lukewarm.

3. In a small bowl or cup, whisk the warm water and yeast until the yeast dissolves. Stir the yeast into the milk mixture.

4. Add the egg and stir to combine.

5. Stir the flour into the yeast mixture, ½ cup at a time, until it forms a soft dough. Turn the dough out onto a floured surface (or a silicone baking mat), adding more flour as necessary to prevent it from getting tacky, and knead for 10 minutes. Transfer the dough to the oiled bowl, cover loosely with a clean kitchen towel, and let rise for 1 hour.

6. Turn the dough out onto a floured surface (or a silicone baking mat) and roll it into a 12-by-16-inch rectangle, ¼ inch thick. Cut the dough into 48 2-by-2-inch squares. Roll each square into a ball with your hands, dunk each into the sugar coating, covering completely, and place in the Dutch oven. Cover loosely with a clean kitchen towel and let rise for 1 hour.

7. Preheat the oven to 350°F.

8. Bake the bread for 25 minutes. Cover loosely with aluminum foil and bake for 30 minutes.

TO MAKE THE GLAZE

1. While the monkey bread bakes, in a small saucepan over low heat, warm the butter, dark brown sugar, honey, water, cinnamon, and ginger, stirring frequently.

2. When the monkey bread comes out of the oven, pour the glaze evenly over it and let sit for 10 minutes. Serve warm.

VARIATION TIP: Add 1 cup of crushed pecans to the glaze.

ICED BLUEBERRY BISCUITS

MAKES 7 / PREP TIME: 15 MINUTES / COOK TIME: 15 MINUTES
CAST IRON: BISCUIT PAN

As one of the captains of the high school swim team, I spent many mornings up before sunrise, swimming laps in downtown Durham's YMCA. After an hour of drills and repetitions, we'd get dressed and head out for breakfast before school. Breakfast was always biscuits. Biscuits with butter and honey, biscuit sandwiches, dessert biscuits. When I left the South for college, homemade blueberry biscuits became a special treat on the days I was feeling especially homesick. To this day, a warm and glazed blueberry biscuit tastes like home.

FOR THE BISCUITS
½ cup (1 stick) cold salted butter, cubed, plus more for the pan
2 cups all-purpose flour
1 teaspoon baking soda
1 teaspoon baking powder
1 teaspoon sea salt

1 cup buttermilk
1 cup fresh blueberries

FOR THE ICING
1 cup confectioners' sugar
1 tablespoon water

TO MAKE THE BISCUITS

1. Preheat the oven to 425°F.

2. Grease each well in the biscuit pan with butter and set aside.

3. In a large bowl, mix the flour, baking soda, baking powder, and sea salt.

4. Add the cold butter cubes to the flour mixture. Mix together with your hands, crumbling the butter, until the texture resembles coarse cornmeal.

5. Stir in the buttermilk and the blueberries. The mixture should form a soft dough.

6. Divide the dough evenly among the wells in the prepared pan.

7. Bake for 15 minutes, or until cooked through and golden brown.

1. While the biscuits bake, in a small bowl, whisk the confectioners' sugar and water.

2. Remove the biscuits from the pan and brush with the glaze. Serve warm.

   VARIATION TIP: To the glaze, add 1 teaspoon of lemon extract, or replace the water with 1 tablespoon of freshly squeezed lemon juice to give it a citrusy twist.

YEASTED APPLE CIDER DONUTS

MAKES 12 / PREP TIME: 45 MINUTES / INACTIVE TIME: 3 HOURS
COOK TIME: 20 MINUTES
CAST IRON: 12-INCH SKILLET OR DUTCH OVEN

Autumn will always remind me of the years I spent living in Baltimore, the way the cool air swept through the city breathing new life into everything. Something about living in a city amplifies the changing of the seasons, and everything about fall in Baltimore felt magical. Nowadays, as soon as the temperature dips slightly below oppressively hot, I wish I was wandering through Baltimore's farmers' market with an apple cider donut in hand.

FOR THE DONUTS
Olive oil, for the bowl
1 cup apple cider
4 tablespoons salted butter
½ cup buttermilk
2 teaspoons active dry yeast
2 eggs, lightly beaten
1 teaspoon vanilla extract
4 cups all-purpose flour,
    plus more for rolling

½ cup sugar
1 teaspoon baking powder
1 tablespoon baking soda
1 teaspoon ground cinnamon
1 teaspoon ground nutmeg
Pinch sea salt
Peanut oil or coconut oil, for frying

FOR THE GLAZE
¼ cup apple cider
2 cups confectioners' sugar

TO MAKE THE DONUTS

1. Coat a large bowl with olive oil and set aside.

2. In a small saucepan over medium-low heat, simmer the apple cider for about 30 minutes until it reduces by half. Remove from the heat.

3. Stir in the butter and let cool until lukewarm.

4. Stir in the buttermilk, yeast, eggs, and vanilla. Cover and let sit for 10 minutes.

5. In a large bowl, mix the flour, sugar, baking powder, baking soda, cinnamon, nutmeg, and sea salt.

6. Add the cider mixture to the flour mixture and stir until it forms a loose dough. Transfer the dough to the oiled bowl, cover loosely with a clean kitchen towel, and let rise for 2 hours.

7. Turn the dough out onto a floured surface (or a silicone baking mat), coating the dough with flour until it is no longer sticky, and pat the dough flat into a 12-by-16-inch rectangle. Fold it in half. Repeat patting and folding 8 to 10 times.

8. Roll the dough flat to ¼ inch thick. Use a donut cutter (or a 4-inch and a 1-inch round cookie cutter) to cut the donuts. Transfer the donuts and holes to a sheet of wax paper. Cover loosely with a clean kitchen towel and refrigerate for 1 hour.

9. In the skillet over high heat, heat at least 3 inches of oil to 375°F.

10. Fry each donut for 2 minutes per side. Transfer to a wire rack to drain.

TO MAKE THE GLAZE

1. While the donuts fry, in a small bowl, stir together the apple cider and confectioners' sugar, adding the sugar a little at a time, until the glaze is thick enough to coat the back of a spoon.

2. Dunk the drained donuts in the glaze, turning a few times to coat well.

3. Transfer to a drying rack to cool slightly. Serve warm.

VARIATION TIP: Substitute ginger beer for the cider in this recipe for a spicy twist!

CINNAMON STREUSEL COFFEE CAKE

SERVES 6 TO 8 / PREP TIME: 20 MINUTES / COOK TIME: 45 MINUTES
CAST IRON: 12-INCH SKILLET

Christmas morning with my mom's family is an exquisite affair. Everyone rushes down the stairs to begin the slow gift-opening ritual, the grown-ups sipping coffee and Southern Comfort while nibbling warm slices of Grammy's coffee cake. Later in the day comes a big, multicourse meal. The morning, however, is always my favorite part; I can't think of a more fitting dish to start the festivities with than coffee cake.

FOR THE FILLING
1½ cups packed brown sugar
1 cup chopped pecans
½ cup all-purpose flour
½ cup (1 stick) salted butter,
    at room temperature
2 tablespoons ground cinnamon
1 tablespoon ground ginger
1 tablespoon ground cloves

FOR THE CAKE
3 cups all-purpose flour
2 teaspoons baking powder
1 teaspoon sea salt
1 cup (2 sticks) salted butter,
    at room temperature
1 cup granulated sugar
1 teaspoon vanilla extract
3 eggs
1½ cups whole milk

TO MAKE THE FILLING

In a medium bowl, stir together the brown sugar, pecans, flour, butter, cinnamon, ginger, and cloves. Set aside.

TO MAKE THE CAKE

1. Preheat the oven to 350°F.

2. In a medium bowl, mix the flour, baking powder, and sea salt.

3. In a large bowl, with a wooden spoon or hand mixer, cream together the butter and granulated sugar until light and fluffy. Stir in the vanilla, then add the eggs one at a time, stirring well after each addition.

4. Add the flour mixture and the milk, alternately in thirds, to the butter mixture, stirring well after each addition, until completely combined.

5. Pour half the batter into the skillet. Top with half the filling. Layer the remaining batter on top. Crumble the remaining filling evenly over the top.

6. Bake for 40 to 45 minutes, or until cooked through. Serve hot with a cup of coffee (Southern Comfort optional).

NO-KNEAD DUTCH OVEN BREAD

**SERVES 4 TO 6 / PREP TIME: 15 MINUTES / INACTIVE TIME: 12 HOURS
COOK TIME: 45 MINUTES
CAST IRON: DUTCH OVEN**

The promise of "no-knead bread" seems too good to be true. Bread making has the reputation of being a complicated process that is hard to master. I once spent an entire year baking my way through *The Bread Baker's Apprentice: Mastering the Art of Extraordinary Bread* by Peter Reinhart, so the idea that I could stir some ingredients together, bake without kneading, and end up with bread left me with some questions. It turns out that the key to successful no-knead bread is time. Left for 12 hours to rise, the dough slowly ferments, and the result is crispy and crunchy on the outside and warm and soft on the inside.

2 tablespoons olive oil,
plus more for the bowl
4 cups all-purpose flour

2 teaspoons sea salt
1 teaspoon active dry yeast
2 cups warm water

1. Coat a large bowl with olive oil and set aside.

2. In another large bowl, mix the flour, sea salt, and yeast.

3. Pour the warm water over the flour mixture and stir well to incorporate. Transfer the dough to the oiled bowl, cover loosely with a clean kitchen towel, and let rise for 12 hours or overnight.

4. Preheat the oven to 450°F.

5. Adjust an oven rack to the middle position, and put the Dutch oven in while the oven heats up.

6. Transfer the dough to the warmed Dutch oven. Cover the pot and return it to the oven for 40 minutes.

7. Remove the lid and bake for 15 minutes, until browned on top and baked through.

8. Let cool before slicing and serving warm.

VARIATION TIP: Mix 2 tablespoons of fresh herbs, such as rosemary leaves, thyme, or oregano, into the dough for an easy herbed bread.

PARMESAN PRETZEL ROLLS

MAKES 10 / PREP TIME: 20 MINUTES / INACTIVE TIME: 2 HOURS
COOK TIME: 40 MINUTES
CAST IRON: 12-INCH SKILLET

I spent a long time wondering what magic made pretzels so delicious before real-izing it's not magic—it's science. The process of dropping the dough into a boiling alkaline bath gelatinizes the starch on the outside of the roll, making it a bit gummy and giving pretzels their signature flavor and texture. While "boiling alka-line bath" might sound intimidating, it's as simple as water, baking soda, and salt.

FOR THE DOUGH
Olive oil, for oiling the bowl
1 cup whole milk
2 tablespoons sugar
2 tablespoons shortening
1 teaspoon sea salt
¼ cup warm water
1 tablespoon active dry yeast
1 egg, beaten
2 cups bread flour,
    plus more for kneading

2 tablespoons melted salted butter,
    plus salted butter at room
    temperature for the skillet
½ cup grated Parmesan cheese,
    divided

FOR THE PRETZEL ROLLS
6 cups water
¼ cup baking soda
2 tablespoons sea salt, divided

TO MAKE THE DOUGH

1. Coat a large bowl with olive oil and set aside.

2. In a medium saucepan over medium-high heat, scald the milk, bringing it almost to a boil, and remove it from the heat.

3. Stir in the sugar, shortening, and 1 teaspoon of sea salt, and let cool until lukewarm.

4. In a small bowl or cup, whisk the warm water and yeast until the yeast dissolves. Stir the yeast into the milk mixture.

5. Add the egg and stir to combine.

6. Stir the flour into the yeast mixture, ½ cup at a time, until it forms a soft dough. Turn the dough out onto a floured surface (or a silicone baking mat), adding more flour as necessary to prevent it from getting tacky, and knead for 10 minutes. Transfer the dough to the oiled bowl, cover loosely with a clean kitchen towel, and let rise for 1 hour.

7. Grease the skillet with butter.

8. Divide the dough into 10 pieces. Form each piece into a ball by pinching the dough at the base so the top is tight. Cluster the balls together in the skillet, pinched-side down. Cover loosely with a clean kitchen towel and let rise for 1 hour.

TO MAKE THE PRETZEL ROLLS

1. In a large pot over high heat, bring the water to a boil.

2. Stir in the baking soda and 1 tablespoon of sea salt, and stir until dissolved.

3. Drop the balls into the boiling water, one at a time, and flip after 30 seconds and boil for 30 seconds more. With a slotted spoon, transfer them to the skillet.

4. With kitchen scissors or a sharp knife, cut an X in the top of each roll.

5. Sprinkle each roll with a bit of the remaining 1 tablespoon of sea salt and ¼ cup of Parmesan cheese.

6. Bake for 25 to 30 minutes until cooked through and browned.

7. Brush the rolls with the melted butter and top with the remaining ¼ cup of Parmesan cheese. Serve warm.

PREPARATION TIP: If you feel adventurous, make pretzel knots instead of rolls. Instead of shaping the dough into balls, roll the dough into 6-inch-long ropes and tie them into knots. Proceed with the recipe as written.

BISCUITS & GRAVY

SERVES 4 / PREP TIME: 20 MINUTES / COOK TIME: 15 MINUTES
CAST IRON: BISCUIT PAN AND 12-INCH SKILLET

Fluffy, buttery biscuits topped with a creamy, peppery sausage gravy are on the short list of my all-time favorite diner breakfasts (right up there with plate-size pancakes and hash browns). Key to the whole experience is the traditional sausage gravy spiced with a generous amount of black pepper. Served with a hot plate of scrambled eggs and a steaming cup of coffee, this is the epitome of a hearty breakfast.

FOR THE BISCUITS
1 cup all-purpose flour
½ teaspoon baking soda
½ teaspoon baking powder
½ teaspoon sea salt
4 tablespoons cold salted butter, cubed, plus more for the pan
½ cup buttermilk

FOR THE GRAVY
6 ounces ground pork sausage
2 garlic cloves, minced
2 tablespoons all-purpose flour
1 cup whole milk
½ teaspoon sea salt
1 teaspoon freshly ground black pepper

TO MAKE THE BISCUITS

1. Preheat the oven to 425°F.

2. In a medium bowl, mix the flour, baking soda, baking powder, and sea salt.

3. Add the cold butter cubes to the flour mixture. Mix together with your hands, crumbling the butter, until the texture resembles coarse cornmeal.

4. Stir in the buttermilk.

5. Grease each well in the biscuit pan with butter. Divide the dough evenly among the wells of the pan.

6. Bake for 15 minutes, or until cooked through and golden brown.

1. While the biscuits bake, in the skillet over medium-high heat, cook the sausage and garlic for 3 to 5 minutes until the sausage is browned.

2. Stir in the flour and continue cooking until it is fully incorporated.

3. Whisk in the milk, whisking quickly until the gravy thickens and bubbles.

4. Season with the sea salt and pepper.

5. Top each biscuit with gravy and serve warm.

VARIATION TIP: For a spicy alternative, make the gravy with chorizo or hot Italian sausage.

WHITE CHEDDAR IRISH SODA BREAD

SERVES 4 TO 6 / PREP TIME: 15 MINUTES / COOK TIME: 40 MINUTES
CAST IRON: 12-INCH SKILLET

My youngest sister, Genevieve, moved to Ireland after graduating college and appears to have absolutely no intention of moving back. So we are left with the horrible burden of having to visit her, something I did for the first time a few years ago with my stepmom and sister Lauren. We spent a week exploring Dublin and Galway, drinking Guinness and whiskey, getting our money's worth from our rain slickers, and eating as much soda bread as we could get our hands on. Irish soda bread is, as the name implies, bread made with baking soda. Soda bread is a quick bread that was born from need, as it comes together quickly with minimal ingredients. In fact, a traditional soda bread is made simply from flour, baking soda, and buttermilk—the buttermilk and baking soda react to provide the leavening. While this recipe is prepared in a cast iron skillet in the traditional style, I've adapted it slightly with the addition of an egg, butter, and Cheddar cheese.

2 cups all-purpose flour,
 plus more for rolling
1½ teaspoons baking powder
1 teaspoon baking soda
1 teaspoon sea salt
1 cup shredded white Cheddar
 cheese, divided

½ cup (1 stick) cold salted butter,
 cubed, plus more for the pan
1 egg
1 cup buttermilk
2 tablespoons minced fresh chives
Irish butter, for serving
Jam of choice, for serving

1. Preheat the oven to 375°F.

2. In a large bowl, mix the flour, baking powder, baking soda, sea salt, and ¾ cup of Cheddar cheese.

3. Add the cold butter cubes to the flour mixture. Mix together with your hands, crumbling the butter, until the texture resembles coarse cornmeal.

4. In a small bowl, whisk the egg and buttermilk.

5. Stir the egg mixture into the flour mixture, stirring until it forms a ball. Turn the dough out onto a floured surface (or a silicone baking mat). Pat the dough out flat and fold it a few times, eventually forming it into a rough ball the size of the skillet.

6. Grease the sides and bottom of the skillet. Transfer the dough to the skillet.

7. With kitchen scissors or a sharp knife, cut a big X across the top of the dough. Top the dough with the remaining ¼ cup of Cheddar cheese and the chives.

8. Bake for 35 to 40 minutes, or until cooked through and golden brown.

9. Slice and serve with a pat of Irish butter and jam.

VARIATION TIP: Add 1 tablespoon of caraway seeds and 1 tablespoon of fennel seeds to the dough for a seeded version of this classic Irish bread.

CHAPTER 4

FIXIN'S

SPICY BOILED PEANUTS

SERVES 4 TO 6 / PREP TIME: 5 MINUTES / COOK TIME: 3 TO 5 HOURS
CAST IRON: DUTCH OVEN
(USE ONLY AN ENAMELED DUTCH OVEN FOR THIS RECIPE BECAUSE UNENAMELED
CAST IRON WILL BE DAMAGED BY SIMMERING WATER.)

When green peanut season arrives in the late summer, roadside stands across the South are flooded with boiled peanuts. Signs dotting country roads advertise HOT SPICY BOILED PEANUTS. When you pull over, you'll be offered a bag of "bald peanuts," spooned out of a piping-hot 10-gallon pot, spiced to perfection and ready to eat. I love serving boiled peanuts when we smoke a pork shoulder. Nothing beats sitting around popping peanuts, drinking a cold beer, and relaxing.

1 pound raw peanuts
   in the shell, washed
2 quarts water
½ cup sea salt

1 tablespoon red pepper flakes
1 tablespoon ground
   chipotle chile pepper
1 tablespoon cayenne pepper

1. In a large pot over medium-low heat, combine the peanuts, water, sea salt, red pepper flakes, chipotle pepper, and cayenne pepper. Simmer for at least 3 hours, or up to 5, until the peanuts are tender.

2. Drain and serve.

INGREDIENT TIP: Omit the spices for an equally delicious, if slightly more gentle, peanut experience.

GARLIC SMASHED POTATOES

**SERVES 4 / PREP TIME: 10 MINUTES / COOK TIME: 1 HOUR, 15 MINUTES
CAST IRON: 10-INCH SKILLET**

Smashed potatoes combine everything that is great about mashed potatoes with everything that is great about roasted potatoes. There is something irresistible about the crisp potato edge in all its buttery, garlicky glory. For a delicious dinner, serve them with a rare steak, an arugula salad, and a glass of red wine.

7 to 10 small or medium red potatoes
¼ cup olive oil, divided
1 teaspoon sea salt, divided
1 teaspoon red pepper flakes, divided

Freshly ground black pepper
4 tablespoons salted butter, cubed
3 garlic cloves, minced

1. Preheat the oven to 350°F.

2. In the skillet, toss the potatoes with 2 tablespoons of olive oil, ½ teaspoon of sea salt, ½ teaspoon of red pepper flakes, and a pinch of black pepper.

3. Roast for 30 minutes, or until a fork easily penetrates the potatoes.

4. Increase the oven temperature to 425°F.

5. With a potato masher or fork, smash the potatoes flat. Return to the oven and roast for 25 minutes.

6. Flip the potatoes, and top with the remaining 2 tablespoons of olive oil, the butter cubes, the remaining ½ teaspoon of sea salt, the remaining ½ teaspoon of red pepper flakes, a pinch of black pepper, and the garlic. Roast for 15 to 20 minutes, until cooked through, brown, and crisp.

PREPARATION TIP: Smashed potatoes are *always* delicious, but this dish really shines when the potatoes are freshly dug. Look for fresh potatoes in your farmers' market during late summer and early fall.

PUMPKIN & ACORN SQUASH GRATIN

SERVES 4 TO 6 / PREP TIME: 30 MINUTES / COOK TIME: 45 MINUTES
CAST IRON: 12-INCH SKILLET

This pumpkin and squash gratin, a twist on a traditional potato gratin, has become the surprise star of our Thanksgiving table. The squash brings just enough sweetness to the dish, balancing the rich flavors of cream and cheese. Finish with a dash of red pepper flakes and serve what surely will be the star of your show.

1½ cups heavy (whipping) cream
2 garlic cloves, minced
Pinch red pepper flakes
Sea salt
1 small Sugar Pie pumpkin, or butternut squash, peeled, cored, halved, and cut in ⅛-inch thick slices, divided

1 cup shredded Asiago cheese, divided
1 small acorn squash, peeled, cored, halved, and cut in ½-inch thick slices, divided
8 ounces white Cheddar cheese, grated, divided

1. Preheat the oven to 350°F.

2. In a small pot, combine the cream, garlic, red pepper flakes, and a pinch of sea salt. Over medium-high heat, scald the cream by bringing it almost to a boil, and then remove it from the heat. Set aside.

3. In the skillet, layer one-third of the pumpkin, sprinkle with ⅓ cup of Asiago cheese, layer one-third of the squash, and sprinkle with one-third of the Cheddar cheese. Repeat 2 more times, ending with a layer of Cheddar cheese.

4. Sprinkle the top with sea salt.

5. Pour the garlic cream over the gratin.

6. Bake for 45 minutes, or until bubbling and browned.

VARIATION TIP: Add ribbons of chard to the layers for a green, vitamin-rich variation.

BROWN BUTTER SWEET CARROTS

SERVES 4 TO 6 / PREP TIME: 15 MINUTES / COOK TIME: 55 MINUTES
CAST IRON: 12-INCH SKILLET

Sweet carrots have always been a holiday staple in my family, and for good reason. Slow cooked in butter and brown sugar, these carrots are addictive. Over the years, I've made variations using rainbow carrots (nothing is more beautiful than a medley of purple, orange, and white carrots), adding purple and golden beets, or substituting raw honey for the brown sugar. The sweetness pairs nicely with tangy, heavy meat dishes, making these a favorite side dish to serve with Dutch Oven Pulled Pork (page 144) or Seared Duck Breast with Apple Cider (page 131).

½ pound thick-cut bacon, chopped
4 tablespoons salted butter
12 to 15 large carrots, cut into
   ½-inch slices

¼ cup packed brown sugar
2 garlic cloves, minced
Pinch sea salt
Pinch red pepper flakes

1. In the skillet over medium-low heat, combine the bacon and butter. Cook for about 10 minutes, stirring frequently, until the bacon browns slightly.

2. Add the carrots, brown sugar, garlic, sea salt, and red pepper flakes. Stir to coat the carrots thoroughly with bacon drippings and butter.

3. Simmer, uncovered, for 45 minutes, stirring occasionally, or until the carrots soften but are still firm.

VARIATION TIP: Try a variation of this dish by simmering the carrots in 1 cup of bone broth with 2 tablespoons of butter, a pinch of sea salt, and a minced garlic clove. My son loves it.

SAUERKRAUT & DUMPLINGS

SERVES 4 / PREP TIME: 20 MINUTES / COOK TIME: 1 HOUR, 10 MINUTES
CAST IRON: 12-INCH SKILLET

This recipe comes from my great-grandmother Flossie. It's a simple recipe, but full of complex flavor. I've spent a lot of time tracing the origins of this recipe by talking to food historians and family members. Flossie and her husband both came from Scots-Irish families with deep roots in the North Carolina mountains. The region was also home to many German immigrants, and variations of sauerkraut and dumplings, usually served with pork, are common within German communities. So, so my best guess is that as the immigrant communities merged and blended, the exchange of food and culture brought this recipe to my family.

FOR THE SAUERKRAUT
1 head cabbage, thinly shredded
2 cups apple cider vinegar
1 tablespoon caraway seeds
1 teaspoon mustard seeds
1 teaspoon ground ginger
1 teaspoon ground cinnamon
1 teaspoon cayenne pepper

FOR THE DUMPLINGS
1 cup buttermilk
1 egg, beaten
1 cup all-purpose flour
½ teaspoon sea salt
½ teaspoon baking soda

TO MAKE THE SAUERKRAUT

1. In the skillet over medium-low heat, combine half the shredded cabbage with the apple cider vinegar. Simmer for 10 minutes.

2. Add the remaining cabbage, the caraway seeds, mustard seeds, ginger, cinnamon, and cayenne pepper. Stir to combine and simmer for 30 minutes more, stirring frequently.

TO MAKE THE DUMPLINGS

1. In a large bowl, whisk the buttermilk, egg, flour, sea salt, and baking soda. Drop spoonfuls of the dough over the hot sauerkraut and cover.

2. Cook for 30 minutes. Once the dumplings have set, serve hot.

    SERVING TIP: This sauerkraut is quick and easy—make it without the dumplings and serve alongside a pork roast or add to a bowl of butternut squash soup!

ACCORDION POTATOES

SERVES 5 / PREP TIME: 15 MINUTES / COOK TIME: 1 HOUR
CAST IRON: 12-INCH SKILLET

Sliced baked potatoes, also known as Hasselback potatoes, are served sliced but still whole. You slice them *almost* all the way through, allowing them to absorb the seasoning and crisp to perfection. It's somewhere between a baked potato and a fried potato, with a little essence of mashed potato thrown in. When making them I like to employ a two-step approach: Start them in the oven topped with butter, and halfway through baking, top them with olive oil once the potatoes have cooked and fanned out slightly. This recipe is simple, but feel free to experiment with toppings. Add cheese, bacon, fresh herbs—whatever strikes your fancy!

5 Yukon gold potatoes, cut crosswise into ½ inch (or thinner) slices, stopping short of cutting through the bottom skin (see Preparation Tip)

½ cup (1 stick) salted butter, cubed
4 garlic cloves, minced
1 tablespoon sea salt
1 teaspoon red pepper flakes
2 tablespoons olive oil

1. Preheat the oven to 425°F.

2. Arrange the potatoes in the skillet.

3. Sprinkle the butter cubes over the potatoes, followed by the garlic, sea salt, and red pepper flakes.

4. Bake for 30 minutes.

5. Brush with the olive oil and bake for 30 minutes more.

PREPARATION TIP: When slicing, take care not to slice all the way through the bottom skin. Slice slowly, stopping your knife with ⅛ inch to go.

GOAT'S MILK & PIMENTO CHEESE SQUASH BLOSSOMS

SERVES 8 TO 10 / PREP TIME: 20 MINUTES / COOK TIME: 15 MINUTES
CAST IRON: 12-INCH SKILLET OR DUTCH OVEN

For the past few years I have had the pleasure of working with a local farm, Greenlands, to help produce seasonal farm-to-fork dinners. They feature foods straight from the field served in the farmhouse dining room. I relish the opportunity to whip up some of my favorite local and seasonal meals for an audience I know will truly appreciate this fresh, quality produce, meat, and dairy. One inspired dish was squash blossoms stuffed with pimento cheese and fried in a goat's milk batter. Pimento cheese, a classic Southern spread, provides an interesting twist on the classic stuffed squash blossom, and goat's milk batter brings a tanginess to the dish that also lightens it. The result is crunchy, gooey, and a very big hit.

FOR THE PIMENTO CHEESE

2 cups shredded extra-sharp
    Cheddar cheese
4 ounces diced pimientos
2 tablespoons mayonnaise

FOR THE STUFFED BLOSSOMS

24 squash blossoms
Peanut oil or sunflower oil, for frying
2 cups all-purpose flour
2 teaspoons sea salt
2 teaspoons cayenne pepper
3 cups goat's milk

TO MAKE THE PIMENTO CHEESE

In a food processor (or blender), combine the Cheddar cheese, pimientos, and mayonnaise. Pulse until thoroughly combined.

TO MAKE THE STUFFED BLOSSOMS

1. Stuff each squash blossom with 1 tablespoon of pimento cheese and crimp the end of the petals around the cheese to secure it.

2. In the skillet over high heat, heat 1 inch of peanut oil to 375°F.

3. In a large bowl, whisk the flour, sea salt, and cayenne pepper.

4. Slowly add the goat's milk, a little at a time, stirring to combine until the consistency resembles pancake batter. It should be thin enough to pour but not soupy.

5. Dip each stuffed blossom in the batter so the bloom is coated almost to the stem.

6. Fry in the hot oil for 2 to 3 minutes per side. (You may need to do this in batches to avoid crowding the skillet.) Transfer to a wire rack. Cool slightly and serve immediately.

PREPARATION TIP: Making pimento cheese is a great task for kids in the kitchen. Combine all the ingredients in a resealable plastic bag and let them squeeze and mash to incorporate.

ROASTED BRUSSELS SPROUTS
WITH BACON JAM

SERVES 4 / PREP TIME: 10 MINUTES / COOK TIME: 1 HOUR, 45 MINUTES
CAST IRON: 10-INCH SKILLET

I first had bacon jam at a local restaurant that spearheaded the "farm-to-table" movement in our area. It was served on a big stack of fried green tomatoes and pimento cheese. As I walked home, all I could think about was bacon jam, and I was determined to make a batch of my own. My favorite way to serve it is with Brussels sprouts, especially for people who say, "I hate Brussels sprouts," and I have a pretty high conversion rate. Something about the combination of crisp edges, smoky bacon, and tender sprouts brings out the best of all the flavors, and makes this a dish I come back to time and again.

1 tablespoon salted butter
1 white onion, diced
2 garlic cloves, minced
1 pound thick-cut bacon,
    roughly chopped
¼ cup packed brown sugar

1 tablespoon apple cider vinegar
1 teaspoon sea salt
Pinch red pepper flakes
24 Brussels sprouts, stems
    trimmed and sprouts halved

1. In a large skillet over medium-low heat, melt the butter.

2. Add the onion, garlic, and bacon. Simmer for 15 to 20 minutes, stirring frequently, or until the onion browns.

3. Stir in the brown sugar, apple cider vinegar, sea salt, and red pepper flakes. Simmer for 40 minutes. Remove from the heat.

4. Preheat the oven to 350°F.

5. Add the Brussels sprouts to the skillet, and toss to coat in the bacon jam.

6. Roast for 40 to 45 minutes, or until tender.

SERVING TIP: The bacon jam is delicious on its own. Try it drizzled on top of a batch of Fried Green Tomatoes (page 80).

NEW YEAR'S DAY SKILLET
OF LUCK & FORTUNE

SERVES 4 / PREP TIME: 15 MINUTES / COOK TIME: 1 HOUR, 45 MINUTES
CAST IRON: 12-INCH SKILLET

Like many Southerners, I grew up eating pork, collard greens, and black-eyed peas on New Year's Day. These foods are traditionally thought to bring luck, prosperity, and good fortune, so being a superstitious person, I wouldn't dare start a new year without them. Over the past few years, I've condensed the three components into one skillet with wonderful results.

1 cup dried black-eyed peas
4 tablespoons salted butter
1 pound thick-cut bacon, diced
1 white onion, diced
3 garlic cloves, minced

1 tablespoon honey
1 bunch fresh collard greens,
    stemmed, leaves sliced into ribbons
¼ cup apple cider vinegar
1 teaspoon sea salt
1 teaspoon cayenne pepper

1. In a medium saucepan over high heat, bring 3 cups of water and the black-eyed peas to a boil. Reduce the heat to low, and cover the pan. Simmer for 1 hour. Remove from the heat and let cool.

2. In the skillet over medium heat, melt the butter.

3. Stir in the bacon, onion, garlic, and honey. Cook for 12 to 15 minutes, stirring frequently, until the bacon and onion brown.

4. Drain the black-eyed peas and add them to the skillet along with the collard greens, apple cider vinegar, sea salt, and cayenne pepper. Stir well to coat the greens. Reduce the heat to low.

5. Simmer for 30 minutes, stirring frequently, until the black-eyed peas are tender.

6. Serve warm.

SERVING TIP: Eat this every year on New Year's Day for good fortune and prosperity!

FRIED GREEN TOMATOES

SERVES 1 TO 2 / PREP TIME: 15 MINUTES / COOK TIME: 15 MINUTES
CAST IRON: 12-INCH SKILLET

When I worked as a museum educator at the Jewish Museum of Maryland, we created an exhibit about Jewish food culture that took an in-depth look at how food has evolved, changed, and adapted. I learned through our research that fried green tomatoes, while popularized in the 1990s by the movie of the same name, have origins far outside the South. Recipes for the dish were first seen in late nineteenth-century Jewish cookbooks in the Northeast and Midwest. Since *Fried Green Tomatoes* made them a dish synonymous with Southern food culture, they have taken on a new life, and can be found everywhere from hole-in-the-wall meat-and-threes to gourmet farm-to-table restaurants. No matter their origins, fried green tomatoes are one of my favorite late-summer dishes.

Peanut oil or safflower oil, for frying

1 cup plus 2 tablespoons all-purpose flour, divided

3 teaspoons paprika, divided

3 teaspoons cayenne pepper, divided

1½ teaspoons ground chipotle chile pepper, divided

1½ teaspoons red pepper flakes, divided

2 eggs

¼ cup apple cider vinegar

1 cup cornmeal

1 large green tomato, halved, and sliced into ½-inch-thick slices

1. In the skillet over high heat, heat 1 inch of peanut oil to 375°F.

2. On a clean work surface, line up 3 small bowls. In the first bowl, whisk 1 cup of flour, 1½ teaspoons of paprika, 1½ teaspoons of cayenne, ¾ teaspoon of chipotle pepper, and ¾ teaspoon of red pepper flakes. In the second bowl, whisk the eggs and apple cider vinegar. In the third bowl, mix the cornmeal and the remaining 2 tablespoons of flour, and 1½ teaspoons of paprika, 1½ teaspoons of cayenne pepper, ¾ teaspoon of chipotle chile pepper, and ¾ teaspoon of red pepper flakes.

3. Dredge the tomato slices in the flour mixture, dip into the egg mixture, and then dredge in the cornmeal mixture.

4. Add them to the hot oil and fry for 2 to 3 minutes per side. Transfer to a wire rack to cool slightly. Repeat with the remaining tomato slices.

5. Serve hot.

VARIATION TIP: Make a batch of hot fried green tomatoes with cinnamon, ginger, and cloves instead of paprika, cayenne pepper, chipotle chile pepper, and red pepper flakes, and try them with vanilla ice cream and caramel sauce.

HUSH PUPPIES

My family used to travel a few times a year from our home in North Carolina's Piedmont region to our family house on the coast. A barbecue place called King's was my grandma's favorite place to stop for lunch on our way to the beach. We'd order barbecue and coleslaw sandwiches, sweet tea, and hush puppies. Their hush puppies, served hot, fresh, and with a pat of butter for dipping, were—and still are—the perfect accompaniment to an eastern North Carolina barbecue sandwich. It's just not a pig pickin' without hush puppies.

FOR THE HONEY BUTTER
4 tablespoons salted butter,
   at room temperature
1 tablespoon honey

FOR THE HUSH PUPPIES
Peanut oil or safflower oil, for frying
1 cup cornmeal

½ cup all-purpose flour
1 teaspoon ground paprika
1 teaspoon cayenne pepper
1 teaspoon garlic powder
½ teaspoon sea salt
1 egg
½ cup buttermilk

TO MAKE THE HONEY BUTTER

In a small bowl, stir together the butter and honey. Set aside.

TO MAKE THE HUSH PUPPIES

1. In the skillet over high heat, heat 2 inches of peanut oil to 375°F.

2. In a medium bowl, mix the cornmeal, flour, paprika, cayenne pepper, garlic powder, and sea salt.

3. In a small bowl, whisk the egg and buttermilk. Fold the egg mixture into the cornmeal mixture. With your hands, form 18 to 20 1-inch balls.

4. Drop each ball into the hot oil. Cook for 2 to 3 minutes per side until browned and cooked through. Transfer to a wire rack to cool. (You may want to do this in batches so you don't crowd the skillet.) Cook the remaining balls.

5. Serve warm with the honey butter.

VARIATION TIP: Add a few tablespoons of minced jalapeño chile pepper to the batter for a spicy twist.

FRIED PLANTAINS WITH CINNAMON & HONEY

SERVES 4 / PREP TIME: 5 MINUTES / COOK TIME: 10 MINUTES
CAST IRON: GRIDDLE

One of my best friends, Kellie, is from Trinidad. Over the years she's introduced me to some of her favorite Trinidadian foods, from doubles to plantains. Fried plantains have become a favorite treat because they are quick, easy, and intensely satisfying. My favorite way to prepare them is to panfry them quickly in butter with a bit of cinnamon. Served hot with a drizzle of honey, they work well as a side dish with main courses like the Pork Porterhouse (page 140), but are equally good spooned over Dutch Baby Pancake with Strawberries and Honey (page 25) or Chocolate Buttermilk Stout Pancakes (page 26).

2 ripe plantains, cut ½ inch thick
1 teaspoon ground cinnamon

2 tablespoons salted butter
¼ cup honey

1. In a medium bowl, put the plantains and sprinkle them with cinnamon.

2. On the griddle over medium-high heat, melt the butter.

3. Add the plantains and cook for 3 to 4 minutes per side.

4. Serve hot with the honey to dip.

SERVING TIP: Serve with chocolate gelato instead of honey for a doubly delicious dessert.

ZUCCHINI FRITTERS

SERVES 4 / PREP TIME: 20 MINUTES / INACTIVE TIME: 30 MINUTES
COOK TIME: 15 MINUTES
CAST IRON: 10-INCH SKILLET

Zucchini fritters, like their cousin the latke, are hand-formed patties made from grated zucchini, onion, egg, and a touch of flour. Once drained and given a good squeeze, the zucchini fries up exquisitely, crisping along the edges just right and holding together well. These fritters are delicious served like latkes with sour cream and applesauce, topped with an egg for breakfast, or even on top of a burger (page 151).

1 medium zucchini, grated
1 small white onion, grated
2 garlic cloves, minced
1 egg

¼ cup all-purpose flour
½ teaspoon sea salt
4 tablespoons salted butter

1. In a fine-mesh strainer set over a bowl or the sink, combine the zucchini, onion, and garlic. Let sit for 30 minutes for the zucchini to drain. Transfer to a large bowl.

2. Add the egg, flour, and sea salt and stir to combine.

3. In the skillet over medium-high heat, melt the butter.

4. With your hands, form the zucchini mixture into 8 patties, squeezing out any excess moisture.

5. Add the patties to the skillet and fry each one for 3 to 4 minutes per side. Transfer to a wire rack to drain. (You may want to cook these in batches so you don't crowd the skillet.) Serve hot.

SERVING TIP: For an easy dipping sauce, whisk 1 cup of plain Greek yogurt with the juice of 1 lemon and a few sprigs of fresh dill.

MACARONI 'N' CHEESE

SERVES 8 TO 10 / PREP TIME: 15 MINUTES / COOK TIME: 45 MINUTES
CAST IRON: DUTCH OVEN

Mac 'n' cheese is such a classic Southern side dish that it is frequently listed as a "vegetable" in restaurants. After making mac 'n' cheese with different cheeses, spices, and noodles, I've come to the conclusion that it is best when made in a Dutch oven. Cast iron works especially well when evenly distributed heat makes a noticeable difference in a recipe. A Dutch oven is unparalleled in its ability to bake the mac 'n' cheese all the way through, producing a gooey, cheesy center and a crusty topping—everything you could want from mac 'n' cheese.

1 pound macaroni

8 ounces fresh mozzarella cheese, cubed

3 cups whole milk

1 cup heavy (whipping) cream

2 garlic cloves, minced

4 tablespoons salted butter

2 tablespoons all-purpose flour

1 cup shredded Swiss cheese

Juice of 1 lemon

1 teaspoon sea salt

1 tablespoon ground chipotle chile pepper

1 teaspoon cayenne pepper

2 cups shredded Parmesan cheese

1. Preheat the oven to 350°F.

2. Cook the macaroni according to the package directions, drain, and transfer to the Dutch oven.

3. Mix the mozzarella into the cooked pasta.

4. In a medium pot over medium-high heat, scald the milk, cream, and garlic by bringing it almost to a boil, then removing it from the heat. Set aside.

5. In another medium pot over medium heat, melt the butter.

6. Whisk the flour into the butter to form a roux (see Preparation Tip on page 143), and continue to whisk to prevent clumps from forming.

7. Still whisking, add the milk mixture to the butter roux, whisking to incorporate.

8. Add the Swiss cheese, whisking constantly until the cheese melts. Remove from the heat and add the lemon juice and sea salt.

9. Pour the cheese sauce over the macaroni.

10. Sprinkle with the chipotle pepper, cayenne pepper, and a pinch of sea salt.

11. Top with the Parmesan cheese.

12. Bake for 35 to 40 minutes, or until browned and bubbling.

PREPARATION TIP: Divide the macaroni among the wells of a biscuit pan for individual mac 'n' cheese servings. Cook in a 350°F oven and check after 25 minutes for doneness.

FRIED OKRA WITH CHIPOTLE AIOLI

SERVES 4 / PREP TIME: 10 MINUTES / COOK TIME: 15 MINUTES
CAST IRON: 10-INCH SKILLET

Okra is great—in fact it is one of my favorite foods. Like Brussels sprouts, it is often misunderstood but is delightful when pickled, fried, roasted, or incorporated into stews and gumbos. Properly prepared, it is deliciously crunchy and full of flavor. And it gets top marks as a healthy vegetable to boot, since it's packed with vitamins and boasts a long history of medicinal uses around the world. Fried okra is popular throughout the South, commonly found at meat-and-three style restaurants along with hush puppies, collards, and mac 'n' cheese. I like my fried okra crisp with a splash of apple cider vinegar, and served hot with chipotle aioli.

FOR THE AIOLI
1 cup mayonnaise
1 tablespoon freshly squeezed
   lemon juice
1 tablespoon ground chipotle
   chile pepper

FOR THE OKRA
Peanut oil or safflower oil, for frying
2 cups all-purpose flour, divided
1 teaspoon sea salt, divided
1 teaspoon cayenne pepper, divided
1 teaspoon garlic powder, divided
2 eggs
¼ cup apple cider vinegar
1 tablespoon hot sauce
½ cup bread crumbs
12 okra, cut into ½-inch pieces

TO MAKE THE AIOLI

In a small bowl, whisk together the mayonnaise, lemon juice, and chipotle pepper. Cover and refrigerate.

TO MAKE THE OKRA

1. In the skillet over high heat, heat 1 inch of peanut oil to 375°F.

2. On a clean work surface, line up 3 small bowls. In the first bowl, mix 1 cup of flour, ½ teaspoon of sea salt, ½ teaspoon of cayenne pepper, and ½ teaspoon of garlic powder. In the second bowl, whisk the eggs, apple cider vinegar, and hot sauce. In the third bowl, mix the bread crumbs and the remaining 1 cup of flour, ½ teaspoon of sea salt, ½ teaspoon of cayenne pepper, and ½ teaspoon of garlic of powder.

3. Dredge the okra slices in the seasoned flour, dip into the egg mixture, and then dip into the seasoned bread crumbs.

4. Add the okra to the skillet and fry for 2 to 3 minutes per side until browned and crisp. Transfer to a wire rack to drain.

5. Serve hot with the aioli.

VARIATION TIP: My favorite expansion of this recipe is to fry sliced, *pickled* okra. It sounds crazy, but trust me!

CHAPTER 5

SEAFOOD

BLUE CRAB-STUFFED MAHI MAHI

SERVES 4 / PREP TIME: 30 MINUTES / COOK TIME: 40 MINUTES
CAST IRON: 12-INCH SKILLET

In North Carolina, the big game fish that you can catch offshore range from marlin and mahi mahi to tuna. Over the years, I've reeled in a lot of Spanish mackerel, a fair amount of fish that had to be returned to the sea, and most notably, a midsize mahi mahi that won me a golden hook from Cap'n Fred, my grandfather's friend and a deep-sea fisherman. I'm convinced that no fish tastes as good as one you've caught yourself, and a prize-winning fish tastes even better.

½ cup (1 stick) salted butter
1 cup dry white wine
4 shallots, thinly sliced
2 garlic cloves, minced
2 cups lump crabmeat
Juice of 2 lemons
1 teaspoon cayenne pepper

1 teaspoon sea salt, plus more
    for finishing
1 teaspoon freshly ground
    black pepper
4 mahi mahi steaks
Handful minced scallions (white
    and light green parts), for finishing

1. In the skillet over medium-low heat, melt the butter.

2. Stir in the white wine, shallots, and garlic. Simmer for 20 minutes.

3. In a medium bowl, mix the crabmeat, lemon juice, cayenne pepper, sea salt, and black pepper.

4. Stir in half of the butter and wine mixture.

5. Preheat the oven to 375°F.

6. Cut a horizontal slit into each mahi mahi steak, going to the edge but not through it. Divide the crabmeat among the steaks, then stuff each cavity. Add the steaks to the skillet, spooning the remaining butter and wine mixture over the top.

7. Bake for 20 minutes, or until the fish is flaky and the crabmeat is browned.

8. Season with sea salt as, top with the scallions, and serve.

SALMON with BUTTER, LEMON & DILL

SERVES 2 / PREP TIME: 5 MINUTES / COOK TIME: 10 MINUTES
CAST IRON: 12-INCH SKILLET

This is one of my favorite ways to enjoy salmon, second only perhaps to lox served on a warm everything bagel. It's easy, straightforward, and when made with fresh salmon, incredibly delicious. I like to serve it with lemon rice and grilled asparagus.

4 tablespoons (½ stick) salted butter
2 garlic cloves, minced
2 salmon fillets, patted dry
1 teaspoon sea salt

1 teaspoon freshly ground
  black pepper
Juice of 1 lemon
Handful chopped fresh dill

1. In the skillet over medium heat, melt the butter.

2. Add the garlic.

3. Season the salmon fillets on both sides with the sea salt and black pepper. Place in the skillet and cook for 3 to 4 minutes. Flip to the other side and cook for 3 to 4 minutes.

4. Turn the broiler to high and finish cooking under the broiler for 2 minutes.

5. Top with the lemon juice and fresh dill.

SERVING TIP: Spoon the butter sauce over the salmon before serving.

FRIED GROUPER BITES

SERVES 4 TO 6 / PREP TIME: 15 MINUTES / COOK TIME: 10 MINUTES
CAST IRON: 12-INCH SKILLET

My family's vacation home, dubbed the Swamp House, has been passed down through generations and is my favorite place on earth—a slice of tranquility and comfort on North Carolina's Crystal Coast. When the family comes together in Morehead City, we are treated to seafood that my dad spears during his SCUBA diving excursions. I still relish in the memory of one particular Christmas, when we feasted on a cornucopia of flounder, triggerfish, tilefish, and grouper. The grouper that day was fried and served in bite-size pieces, with tartar sauce for dipping, and got gobbled up as soon as it came out of the fryer. Nothing beats eating fresh fried fish with the salt air in your nose and the sun on your back.

FOR THE FISH

1 cup bread crumbs
1 cup all-purpose flour
1 teaspoon cayenne pepper
1 teaspoon sea salt
1 teaspoon garlic powder
1 teaspoon freshly ground
　　black pepper
2 eggs
1 tablespoon hot sauce
Peanut or coconut oil, for frying
2 grouper fillets, cut into
　　bite-size pieces

FOR THE TARTAR SAUCE

1 cup mayonnaise
1 tablespoon pickle relish
1 tablespoon minced shallot
Juice of 1 lemon
Sea salt
Freshly ground black pepper

TO MAKE THE FISH

1. In a small bowl, mix the bread crumbs, flour, cayenne pepper, sea salt, garlic powder, and black pepper.

2. In a second small bowl, whisk the eggs and hot sauce.

3. In the skillet over high heat, heat ½ inch of oil to 375°F.

4. Dredge the grouper bites in the egg and then fully coat them with the seasoned bread crumbs.

5. Add to the hot oil and fry for 2 to 3 minutes per side until golden brown. Transfer to a wire rack to drain.

TO MAKE THE TARTAR SAUCE

In a small bowl, mix together the mayonnaise, relish, shallot, and lemon juice. Season with sea salt and black pepper, and serve with the hot grouper bites.

VARIATION TIP: To make a fried grouper sandwich, double the batter recipe and fry the fillets whole for 4 to 5 minutes per side. Serve on a toasted bun with a squeeze of lemon juice and a thick spread of tartar sauce.

BROWN BUTTER & GARLIC SWORDFISH

SERVES 2 / PREP TIME: 5 MINUTES / COOK TIME: 40 MINUTES
CAST IRON: 12-INCH SKILLET

You may have noticed that butter is a frequent flyer in my kitchen. It's the fat I'll always choose, working it into almost everything I make. When butter is slowly melted over low heat, it browns in a way similar to caramelization. Add a little garlic to the skillet and your kitchen will smell like heaven. Browned butter is delicious with almost anything, from steak to baked pears, but it is particularly wonderful when paired with swordfish, a firm and meaty game fish that holds up well when cooked at high temperatures.

½ cup (1 stick) salted butter
2 garlic cloves, minced
1½ lemon, cut into 4 slices

Juice of ½ lemon
4 swordfish steaks
Sea salt

1. In the skillet over medium-low heat, melt the butter.

2. Add the garlic and the 4 lemon slices. Simmer them in the butter for 30 minutes, stirring occasionally.

3. Increase the heat to medium-high. Season the swordfish steaks with sea salt. Add them to the skillet, and cook for 3 to 4 minutes per side.

4. Top each with a sprinkle of the lemon juice, and serve.

INGREDIENT TIP: Wahoo is another big game fish with a similar taste that would do well with this style of preparation.

BLACKENED RED DRUM

SERVES 4 / PREP TIME: 10 MINUTES / COOK TIME: 10 MINUTES
CAST IRON: 10-INCH SKILLET

North Carolina's state fish is the red drum, and since moving back to my home state from Maryland, drum has become one of my favorites to cook. Drum is a firm fish with a moderate flavor, and is particularly delicious when blackened.

1 teaspoon ground
   chipotle chile pepper
1 teaspoon dried oregano
1 teaspoon freshly ground
   black pepper
1 teaspoon sea salt

½ teaspoon cayenne pepper
¼ teaspoon red pepper flakes
4 red drum fillets, skinned and boned
4 tablespoons salted butter, melted
Juice of 1 lemon

1. In a small bowl, stir together the chipotle pepper, oregano, black pepper, sea salt, cayenne pepper, and red pepper flakes. Set aside.

2. Place the dry skillet over medium-high heat.

3. Brush each fillet on both sides with melted butter and carefully coat both sides with the spice mixture.

4. Add the fillets to the hot skillet and cook for 2 to 3 minutes per side, until blackened and cooked through.

5. Drizzle the lemon juice over the fish and serve.

INGREDIENT TIP: Red drum and black drum are cousins and can be used interchangeably in this recipe.

SEAFOOD STEW

SERVES 6 / PREP TIME: 30 MINUTES / COOK TIME: 4 HOURS
CAST IRON: DUTCH OVEN

I am writing this on Christmas Eve in my family's cottage on the marsh, while a pot of seafood stew simmers on the stove. My dad has been working on it all day, adding ingredients, adjusting spices, puttering around the kitchen preparing our holiday feast. Seafood stew is a family favorite, a hearty dish that marries the flavors of spicy sausage, shellfish, and a tomato-based broth. My dad likes to fiddle with his recipe; sometimes cooking down tomatoes for the base, omitting fish stock completely. In years past he's added new or different seafood, or experimented with different vegetables, allowing the stew to change based on what is available and in season. This recipe is the classic I keep coming back to—solid and delicious.

¼ cup olive oil
1 pound hot Italian sausage
4 tablespoons salted butter
3 celery stalks with tender
    greens, chopped
1 white onion, chopped
2 carrots, chopped
4 large Yukon gold potatoes, quartered
¼ pound green beans
1 teaspoon sea salt
1 teaspoon freshly ground
    black pepper

1 teaspoon cayenne pepper
One 4-ounce can tomato paste
Two 16-ounce cans crushed tomatoes
    with the juice
6 cups seafood broth
1 pound cod fillet, roughly chopped
1 pound shrimp, peeled
    and deveined
1 cup clams, fresh and shelled
    or canned in liquid
1 cup oysters, fresh and shelled
    or canned in liquid

1. In the Dutch oven over medium-high heat, heat the olive oil.

2. Add the sausage and sauté for 4 minutes per side until cooked through. Remove from the pot and set aside.

3. Add the butter, celery, and onion to the pot. Cook for 2 to 3 minutes.

4. Add the carrots and potatoes. Cook for 5 minutes.

5. Slice the sausage and return it to the pot, along with the green beans, sea salt, black pepper, and cayenne pepper. Cook for 2 to 3 minutes.

6. Add the tomato paste and stir well. Cook for 3 to 4 minutes, until it caramelizes slightly.

7. Stir in the tomatoes and seafood broth. Reduce the heat to low and simmer for 3 hours, stirring occasionally.

8. Return the heat to medium-high and add the cod, shrimp, clams, and oysters. Stir well and cook for 30 minutes.

9. Discard any unopened shellfish. Season with salt and pepper as needed and serve.

INGREDIENT TIP: Based on availability, substitute another mild white fish such as flounder for the cod.

SUMMER SHRIMP & GRITS
ROASTED TOMATO & BROWNED BUTTER

SERVES 4 / PREP TIME: 20 MINUTES / COOK TIME: 45 MINUTES
CAST IRON: 12-INCH SKILLET

When I first learned to make shrimp and grits, I followed Bill Smith's recipe from *Seasoned in the South*, which he serves at his Chapel Hill restaurant, Crook's Corner. It was my go-to shrimp and grits recipe for years. One summer, however, I had a counter full of overripe tomatoes and decided to change things up, slow cooking them with thick-cut bacon and just a little brown sugar. This dish brings out what is best about late-summer tomatoes, by allowing their sweetness to shine in contrast to the red pepper flakes and the Gouda. The finishing touch of basil gives it a unique summer flair.

FOR THE GRITS
4 cups water
2 cups grits
3 cups whole milk
2 teaspoons sea salt
1 teaspoon freshly ground
  white pepper
1 teaspoon freshly ground
  black pepper
2 tablespoons salted butter
1 cup grated smoked Gouda cheese
Juice of ½ lemon

FOR THE SHRIMP
4 tablespoons salted butter
½ pound thick-cut bacon, chopped
1 yellow onion, chopped
2 garlic cloves, minced
2 large tomatoes or 6 small
  Roma tomatoes, chopped
1 tablespoon packed brown sugar
1 teaspoon red pepper flakes
Pinch ground cinnamon
Pinch sea salt
1 pound shrimp, peeled and deveined
Juice of ½ lemon
Handful fresh basil leaves, minced

TO MAKE THE GRITS

1. In a medium pot over high heat, combine the water and grits. Bring to a boil. Reduce the heat to low.

2. Stir in the milk, sea salt, white pepper, black pepper, and butter. Simmer for 40 to 45 minutes, stirring frequently, as the grits thicken.

3. Stir the Gouda into the grits.

4. Add the lemon juice to the grits. Remove from the heat.

TO MAKE THE SHRIMP

1. While the grits cook, in the skillet over medium-low heat, melt the butter.

2. Add the bacon, onion, and garlic. Cook for 5 to 7 minutes, stirring frequently.

3. Stir in the tomatoes, brown sugar, red pepper flakes, cinnamon, and sea salt. Reduce the heat to low and simmer for 30 minutes, stirring frequently.

4. Increase the heat to medium and add the shrimp to the skillet. Cook for 4 to 5 minutes, stirring frequently, until the shrimp turn pink.

5. Top the shrimp with the lemon juice.

6. Serve the shrimp and tomato sauce over the grits. Garnish with the basil.

INGREDIENT TIP: For more adventurous eaters, try heads-on shrimp. Clean and peel the shrimp body as usual, but leave the heads on to add flavor to the dish.

FALL SHRIMP & GRITS
BRUSSELS SPROUTS & SHALLOTS

SERVES 4 / PREP TIME: 15 MINUTES / COOK TIME: 45 MINUTES
CAST IRON: 12-INCH SKILLET

For me, fall is synonymous with Brussels sprouts. They are the culinary signal that the seasons are changing and winter is coming. For this dish I use thick-cut bacon, applewood-smoked if I can find it. There's something lovely about bacon slowly cooked in butter alongside Brussels sprouts that are crisp around the edges and tender in the center.

FOR THE GRITS
4 cups water
2 cups grits
3 cups whole milk
2 teaspoons sea salt
1 teaspoon freshly ground
    white pepper
1 teaspoon freshly ground
    black pepper
2 tablespoons salted butter
1 cup shredded sharp white
    Cheddar cheese
Juice of 1 lemon

FOR THE SHRIMP
2 tablespoons salted butter
½ pound thick-cut bacon, chopped
10 to 12 Brussels sprouts,
    stemmed and quartered
2 shallots, thinly sliced
2 garlic cloves, minced
2 tablespoons olive oil
½ teaspoon sea salt
1 teaspoon red pepper flakes
1 pound raw shrimp,
    peeled and deveined
½ cup shredded Parmesan cheese,
    for serving

TO MAKE THE GRITS

1. In a medium pot over high heat, combine the water and grits. Bring to a boil. Reduce the heat to low.

2. Stir in the milk, sea salt, white pepper, black pepper, and butter. Simmer for 40 to 45 minutes, stirring frequently, as the grits thicken.

3. Stir in the Cheddar cheese and lemon juice. Remove from the heat.

1. Preheat the oven to 375°F.

2. While the grits cook, in the skillet over medium-low heat, melt the butter.

3. Add the bacon, Brussels sprouts, shallots, and garlic, stirring well to coat with the butter. Cook for 5 minutes.

4. Stir in the olive oil, sea salt, and red pepper flakes, and transfer the skillet to the oven.

5. Roast for 30 minutes until the Brussels sprouts brown and become tender.

6. Return the skillet to the stove top over medium heat, and add the shrimp. Cook for 4 to 5 minutes, stirring frequently, until the shrimp are pink.

7. Serve the shrimp and Brussels sprouts over the grits. Top with the Parmesan cheese.

    VARIATION TIP: Substitute canned coconut milk (with the fat) for the whole milk in the grits.

WINTER SHRIMP & GRITS
COLLARDS & BLACK-EYED PEAS

**SERVES 4 / PREP TIME: 15 MINUTES / INACTIVE TIME: 12 HOURS
COOK TIME: 45 MINUTES
CAST IRON: 12-INCH SKILLET**

I enjoy collards many different ways, but I will always love them best with apple cider vinegar and a dash of red pepper flakes. Traditionally, our family eats collards, black-eyed peas, and pork on New Year's Day (page 79). This is one of my favorites, coming back to it over and over throughout the winter. Incorporating it into shrimp and grits makes this dish a bright spot in an otherwise dreary season.

FOR THE GRITS

4 cups water

2 cups grits

3 cups whole milk

2 teaspoons sea salt

1 teaspoon freshly ground white pepper

1 teaspoon freshly ground black pepper

2 tablespoons salted butter

1 cup grated pepper Jack cheese

Juice of 1 lemon

FOR THE SHRIMP

4 tablespoons salted butter

½ pound thick-cut bacon, chopped

1 yellow onion, chopped

2 garlic cloves, minced

1 bunch collards, stemmed, leaves thinly sliced into ribbons

½ cup apple cider vinegar

1 teaspoon red pepper flakes

1 teaspoon sea salt

1 cup dried black-eyed peas, soaked overnight in water to cover and drained

1 pound raw shrimp, peeled and deveined

TO MAKE THE GRITS

1. In a medium pot over high heat, combine the water and grits. Bring to a boil. Reduce the heat to low.

2. Stir in the milk, sea salt, white pepper, black pepper, and butter. Simmer for 40 to 45 minutes, stirring frequently, as the grits thicken.

3. Stir in the pepper Jack cheese and lemon juice.

TO MAKE THE SHRIMP

1. While the grits cook, in the skillet over medium heat, melt the butter.

2. Add the bacon, onion, and garlic. Cook for 15 minutes until the onion begins to soften and the bacon begins to brown.

3. Stir in the collards, apple cider vinegar, red pepper flakes, and sea salt. Reduce the heat to medium-low.

4. Stir in the black-eyed peas. Cook for 25 minutes, until the peas are tender.

5. Add the shrimp to the skillet and stir well. Increase the heat to medium and cook for 4 to 5 minutes until the shrimp are pink.

6. Serve the shrimp and collards over the grits.

INGREDIENT TIP: If collards aren't readily available, substitute kale or Swiss chard.

SPRING SHRIMP & GRITS
ASPARAGUS & PROSCIUTTO

SERVES 4 / PREP TIME: 20 MINUTES / COOK TIME: 45 MINUTES
CAST IRON: 12-INCH SKILLET

Spring is glorious in the South. In coastal North Carolina, there is a moment in mid to late March when the world erupts in blossoms. Gardens begin to produce more than just winter greens, and the prospect of summer's bounty is imminent. Asparagus is often the first of these vegetables to sprout up. This grits dish, in contrast to the heavier fall and winter versions, is light in flavor. The crispness of the asparagus, the tang of the lemon and goat cheese, and the salt of the prosciutto are a refreshing reminder that spring has come.

FOR THE GRITS
4 cups water
2 cups grits
3 cups whole milk
2 teaspoons sea salt
1 teaspoon freshly ground
    white pepper
1 teaspoon freshly ground
    black pepper
2 tablespoons salted butter
1 cup fresh goat cheese
Juice of 1 lemon

FOR THE SHRIMP
2 tablespoons salted butter
2 garlic cloves, minced
2 shallots, thinly sliced
1 bunch fresh asparagus, stem ends
    removed, chopped
Juice of 2 lemons, divided
1 pound raw shrimp,
    peeled and deveined
¼ pound prosciutto, roughly chopped
¼ cup crumbled goat cheese
1 teaspoon sea salt

TO MAKE THE GRITS

1. In a medium pot over high heat, combine the water and grits. Bring to a boil. Reduce the heat to low.

2. Stir in the milk, sea salt, white pepper, black pepper, and butter. Simmer for 40 to 45 minutes, stirring frequently, as the grits thicken.

3. Stir in the lemon juice. Remove from the heat.

TO MAKE THE SHRIMP

1. While the grits cook, in the skillet over medium heat, melt the butter.

2. Add the garlic and shallots, and sauté for 3 to 4 minutes, until the shallots brown.

3. Add the asparagus and half of the lemon juice. Cook for 5 to 7 minutes, stirring frequently, until the asparagus is tender.

4. Add the shrimp to the skillet. Stir well to combine, and cook for 4 to 5 minutes, until pink.

5. Serve the shrimp and asparagus over the grits. Top with the prosciutto, goat cheese, sea salt, and the remaining lemon juice.

INGREDIENT TIP: Reserve the trimmed asparagus stems for making vegetable stock. I like to keep a bag of scraps like this in the freezer to throw together a quick and easy stock.

SHRIMP, SCALLOPS & CORN WITH ZUCCHINI NOODLES & AVOCADO CREMA

SERVES 2 / PREP TIME: 20 MINUTES / COOK TIME: 15 MINUTES
CAST IRON: 12-INCH SKILLET

When I was diagnosed with celiac disease, I mourned the fact that I would have to cut pasta out of my diet. Thankfully, it happened right around the time spiralized vegetables were taking over the culinary landscape, and my friend Liz gave me a vegetable spiralizer. This dish was one of the first I tried, and has quickly become my favorite way to enjoy zucchini noodles. The zucchini, lime juice, avocado, sweet corn, and shellfish all work together in this lovely late-summer dish.

1 avocado, halved and pitted
1 cup plain Greek yogurt
Juice of 3 limes
2 medium zucchini, spiralized or
   sliced into long thin strips
1 tablespoon salted butter

2 cups fresh corn kernels
1 tablespoon ground
   chipotle chile pepper
Pinch sea salt
10 raw shrimp, peeled and deveined
10 scallops, rinsed and patted dry

1. Into a large bowl, scoop out the avocado flesh and mash it with a fork.

2. Stir in the yogurt and the lime juice.

3. Add the zucchini noodles and toss to coat in the avocado crema. Set aside.

4. In the skillet over medium heat, melt the butter.

5. Add the corn, chipotle pepper, and sea salt. Sauté for 4 to 5 minutes.

6. Add the shrimp to the skillet. Stir well. Cook for 4 to 5 minutes, until pink.

7. Move the shrimp and corn to the side of the skillet. Add the scallops in the center and sear for 2 to 3 minutes per side.

8. Portion the zucchini noodles into bowls, and top with the shrimp, scallops, and corn.

INGREDIENT TIP: Greek yogurt is nice in this dish because it is thick and tangy. However, in a pinch, any unflavored full-fat yogurt will do.

SEARED SCALLOPS

SERVES 4 / PREP TIME: 5 MINUTES / COOK TIME: 5 MINUTES
CAST IRON: 12-INCH SKILLET

A friend is a deep-sea scallop fisherman, which means we are often on the receiving end of a bounty of fresh sea scallops. Harvested from the depths of the sea, scallops can be 2 inches in diameter and up to 1 inch thick. Almost nothing tastes better than a fresh scallop quickly seared in butter, so this recipe keeps it simple. Salt, butter, lemon juice, and a hot skillet.

3 tablespoons salted butter
1 dozen sea scallops, rinsed and
    patted dry

Pinch sea salt
Juice of 1 lemon

1. Place the skillet over medium-high heat.

2. Add the butter to melt.

3. Place the scallops in the skillet. Sprinkle with sea salt and cook for 2 minutes. Flip and cook the other side for 2 minutes.

4. Remove the scallops from the heat, sprinkle with the lemon juice, and serve.

INGREDIENT TIP: If you'd prefer to try this recipe with bay scallops, which are slightly sweeter than sea scallops and quite a bit smaller, reduce the cooking time to 1 minute per side.

PAN-SEARED CRAB CAKES

SERVES 4 / PREP TIME: 15 MINUTES / COOK TIME: 10 MINUTES
CAST IRON: 10-INCH SKILLET

People in my native North Carolina aren't as crab crazy as they are in Maryland, but eight years living in the Old Line State with my husband made us big fans of crab cakes. When we moved back to North Carolina, we were surprised to find that our southern waters were also loaded with crabs—something I had never noticed before! We delighted in the availability of blue crabmeat, and ever since, crab cakes served on sandwiches, salads, or even a bed of zucchini noodles have become a regular part of our dinner menu. They are easy to assemble and feel like a special treat, particularly when pan-seared to perfection.

1 pound lump blue crabmeat
½ cup bread crumbs
1 egg, lightly beaten
Juice of 1 lemon, divided
Zest of 1 lemon
1 tablespoon fresh oregano
   leaves, minced

1 tablespoon fresh
   thyme leaves, minced
1 tablespoon minced fresh chives
Pinch sea salt
Pinch freshly ground black pepper
4 tablespoons salted butter

1. In a large bowl, mix the crabmeat, bread crumbs, egg, half of the lemon juice, the lemon zest, oregano, thyme, chives, sea salt, and black pepper. Form the mixture into 4 crab cakes.

2. In the skillet over medium-high heat, melt the butter.

3. Sear the crab cakes for 4 minutes per side.

4. Top with the remaining lemon juice, and serve.

VARIATION TIP: Add 1 minced jalapeño pepper in lieu of the thyme and oregano for a spicy alternative.

LITTLENECK CLAMS WITH WHITE WINE & BASIL

SERVES 4 / PREP TIME: 25 MINUTES / INACTIVE TIME: 20 MINUTES
COOK TIME: 20 MINUTES
CAST IRON: DUTCH OVEN

It *is* possible to eat clams without drenching them in white wine and butter, but why would you when they are so divine that way? For this dish I prefer sauvignon blanc or pinot grigio; New Zealand whites have a beautiful balance of fruitiness and acidity that complements the buttery saltiness of the clams. I buy two bottles, one to cook with and one to serve chilled with the clams.

2 dozen littleneck clams
½ cup (1 stick) salted butter
3 garlic cloves, minced
2 shallots, thinly sliced

1 teaspoon sea salt
2 cups dry white wine
¼ cup minced fresh basil

1. In a large bowl, cover the clams with cold water. Let sit for 20 minutes to help discharge the silt and sand.

2. In the Dutch oven over medium-low heat, melt the butter.

3. Add the garlic, shallots, and sea salt. Stir well to combine.

4. One at a time, remove the clams from the water (don't dump them in a colander), rinse off any visible debris, and add them to the pot.

5. Stir in the white wine and cover the pot. Cook, covered, for 20 minutes, until the clams open. Discard any unopened clams.

6. Serve the clams in the cooking liquid, topped with the basil.

SERVING TIP: Serve these clams with a loaf of fresh crusty bread for soaking up the wine broth.

CHAPTER 6

POULTRY

BUTTERMILK FRIED CHICKEN

Fried chicken has a long and storied past, and as the simple dish has made its way around the world, its flavors and ingredients have evolved. My favorite is the classic buttermilk fried chicken, with a double-dipped batter and a kick of spice. Soaking the chicken overnight in buttermilk helps keep the meat tender, ensuring its moistness after frying. The double breading creates a nice crisp skin, and grits give a little crunch. Serve fried chicken with Macaroni 'n' Cheese (page 86) and Roasted Brussels Sprouts with Bacon Jam (page 78) for a completely satisfying meal.

FOR THE MARINADE
2 cups buttermilk
1 tablespoon red pepper flakes
1 tablespoon cayenne pepper
1 tablespoon sea salt
1½ teaspoons garlic powder
8 to 10 mixed bone-in, skin-on
  chicken breasts and thighs

FOR THE CHICKEN
3 cups all-purpose flour, divided
1 tablespoon red pepper flakes,
  divided
1 tablespoon cayenne pepper, divided
1 tablespoon sea salt, divided
1½ teaspoons garlic powder, divided
4 eggs
2 tablespoons apple cider vinegar
Peanut oil or coconut oil, for frying
2 cups bread crumbs
¼ cup yellow coarse stone-ground grits

TO MAKE THE MARINADE

1. In a large bowl, mix the buttermilk, red pepper flakes, cayenne pepper, sea salt, and garlic powder.

2. Add the chicken and turn to coat. Cover and soak overnight in the refrigerator.

1. On a clean work surface, line up 3 small bowls. In the first bowl, mix 1½ cups of flour, 1½ teaspoons of red pepper flakes, 1½ teaspoons of cayenne pepper, 1½ teaspoons of sea salt, and ¾ teaspoon of garlic powder. In the second bowl, whisk the eggs and apple cider vinegar. In the third bowl, mix the bread crumbs and the remaining 1½ cups of flour, 1½ teaspoons of red pepper flakes, 1½ teaspoons of cayenne pepper, 1½ teaspoons of sea salt, and ¾ teaspoon of garlic powder.

2. In the skillet over high heat, heat 1 inch of peanut oil to 375°F.

3. Working one piece at a time, dip the chicken into the flour mixture, into the egg mixture, and into the bread crumb mixture.

4. Add to the hot oil and fry: breasts/white meat for 4 to 5 minutes per side; thighs/dark meat for 6 to 7 minutes per side.

5. Transfer to a wire rack to cool slightly before serving.

SERVING TIP: Pop the leftovers in the fridge—cold fried chicken makes the perfect lunch for a summer day on the porch or out at sea.

BISCUIT-TOPPED CHICKEN POTPIE

SERVES 4 / PREP TIME: 45 MINUTES / COOK TIME: 1 HOUR
CAST IRON: 12-INCH SKILLET

Potpies are hearty, filling, and comforting, especially with a biscuit top. The combination of flaky, buttery biscuits and a creamy, rich filling is incomparable. I like to make this dish on a Sunday afternoon because it provides both a filling supper, and leftovers for lunch the next day.

FOR THE CHICKEN FILLING
1 tablespoon olive oil
2 boneless, skinless chicken breasts
2 tablespoons salted butter, divided
5 large carrots, diced
1 Vidalia or other sweet onion, minced
2 garlic cloves, minced
1 cup cremini mushrooms,
    cleaned and sliced
2½ cups whole milk
½ cup heavy (whipping) cream
2 cups butter beans
½ teaspoon ground
    chipotle chile pepper

Sea salt
Freshly ground black pepper
2 tablespoons all-purpose flour

FOR THE BISCUIT TOPPING
2 cups all-purpose flour,
    plus more for shaping
1 teaspoon baking soda
1 teaspoon baking powder
1 teaspoon sea salt
½ cup (1 stick) cold salted
    butter, cubed
1 cup buttermilk

TO MAKE THE CHICKEN FILLING

1. In a skillet over medium heat, heat the oil and cook the chicken for 5 to 6 minutes per side. Remove, chop, and set aside.

2. Return the skillet to medium heat. Add 1 tablespoon of butter and the carrots. Sauté for 3 to 5 minutes.

3. Add the onion and garlic to the skillet. Cook for 5 minutes, until the onion begins to brown.

4. Add the mushrooms. Cook for 4 to 6 minutes, stirring frequently, until they soften.

5. In a medium saucepan over medium-high heat, scald the milk and cream by bringing it almost to a boil and then remove it from the heat. Set aside.

6. Add the butter beans to the skillet, along with the chicken and chipotle chile pepper. Season with sea salt and black pepper. Cook for 2 to 3 minutes, stirring frequently.

7. Add the flour and 1 tablespoon of scalded milk to the skillet. Stir well to incorporate. Continue stirring and slowly pour in the remaining milk.

8. Preheat the oven to 350°F.

TO MAKE THE BISCUIT TOPPING

1. In a medium bowl, mix the flour, baking soda, baking powder, and sea salt.

2. Add the cold butter cubes to the flour mixture. Mix together with your hands, crumbling the butter, until the texture resembles coarse cornmeal.

3. Stir in the buttermilk.

4. Turn the dough out onto a floured work surface (or a silicone baking mat), and pat it out flat into a 12-by-16-inch rectangle about 1 inch thick, sprinkling with a bit of flour to keep the dough from sticking. Fold in half and repeat 3 times. With a biscuit cutter, cut out 10 biscuits. Arrange the biscuits on top of the potpie filling.

5. Bake for 30 to 35 minutes, until the biscuits rise and are cooked through, and the filling is bubbling.

PREPARATION TIP: A friend preferred a top crust instead of individual biscuits. To try this variation, roll the biscuit dough into a 12-inch round and lay it on top of the filling, crimping the edges to the skillet. Be sure to cut slits into the crust for steam to escape!

HOT CHICKEN WINGS

SERVES 2 / PREP TIME: 20 MINUTES / COOK TIME: 15 MINUTES
CAST IRON: 12-INCH SKILLET

After moving to a new town in North Carolina, my husband and I found the best wings we'd ever had at a sports bar called The Copper Penny. They were fried with a double-dip batter and sauced just the right amount. Ever since I found out I have celiac disease, they are one of the things I've missed most, which means they are one of the things I've worked to replicate at home. After a lot of experimenting, I've come up with a recipe that has it all—crisp skin, tender meat, and finger-licking sauce. All ready for you to enjoy from the comfort of your home.

FOR THE BLUE CHEESE DRESSING
½ cup blue cheese
⅓ cup buttermilk
¼ cup sour cream
3 tablespoons mayonnaise
2 tablespoons apple cider vinegar

FOR THE SAUCE
1 cup (2 sticks) salted butter
2 (5-ounce) bottles hot sauce

FOR THE WINGS
Peanut oil or coconut oil, for frying
1 cup all-purpose flour
1 cup bread crumbs
1 tablespoon garlic powder
1 tablespoon sea salt
1 tablespoon red pepper flakes
2 eggs
2 tablespoons apple cider vinegar
12 chicken pieces, wings and
    drumsticks, patted dry
Celery sticks, for serving

TO MAKE THE BLUE CHEESE DRESSING

In a small bowl, stir together the blue cheese, buttermilk, sour cream, mayonnaise, and apple cider vinegar. Cover and refrigerate until needed.

TO MAKE THE SAUCE

In a medium saucepan over medium-low heat, melt the butter. Whisk in the hot sauce. Reduce the heat to low and simmer the sauce while you cook the wings, stirring occasionally.

1. In the skillet over high heat, heat 1 inch of peanut oil to 375°F.

2. On a clean work surface, line up 2 small bowls. In the first bowl, mix the flour, bread crumbs, garlic powder, sea salt, and red pepper flakes. In the second bowl, whisk the eggs and apple cider vinegar.

3. Working one piece at a time, dip the chicken into the egg mixture and then into the flour mixture. Add to the hot oil and fry for 2 to 3 minutes per side.

4. Dunk the cooked chicken in the hot sauce and transfer to a wire rack to cool.

5. Serve with blue cheese dressing for dipping and celery sticks.

PREPARATION TIP: For extra-crispy wings, try a triple-dip batter. Add a third bowl of flour and spices of choice to the assembly line and dip the wings first into the spiced flour, then into the egg mixture, and then into the bread crumbs.

ROAST CHICKEN with ROOT VEGETABLES

SERVES 4 / PREP TIME: 20 MINUTES / COOK TIME: 1 HOUR, 5 MINUTES
CAST IRON: DUTCH OVEN

A tried-and-true recipe for roast chicken is an important part of every cook's arsenal. This chicken is golden brown with crisp skin, tender meat, subtle spice, and butteriness. Roasted over a medley of root vegetables that play off and enhance the flavor of the chicken, it is the type of dish that moves seamlessly from dinner party to Tuesday night.

1 whole chicken, cleaned,
    at room temperature
4 tablespoons salted butter,
    at room temperature
10 garlic cloves, peeled
Sea salt
Freshly ground black pepper

6 medium carrots, roughly chopped
3 beets, purple and golden,
    roughly chopped
3 red potatoes, roughly chopped
1 yellow onion, roughly chopped
¼ cup olive oil

1. Preheat the oven to 475°F.

2. Rub the chicken with the butter, taking care to coat the chicken underneath the skin.

3. Cut 10 small slits in the chicken throughout the body. Fill each slit with 1 garlic clove.

4. Season with sea salt and black pepper.

5. In the bottom of the Dutch oven, put the carrots, beets, potatoes, and onion.

6. Add the olive oil, season with sea salt and black pepper, and toss to coat.

7. Make a bed in the vegetables and nestle the chicken on top.

8. Roast, uncovered, for 20 minutes. Lower the oven temperature to 400°F and continue to roast, uncovered, for 45 minutes.

9. Let the chicken cool slightly before serving.

VARIATION TIP: Use any root vegetables readily available, such as parsnips, radishes, and sweet potatoes.

BARBECUED CHICKEN THIGHS

Like most Southerners, I have strong opinions about barbecue. When it comes to pork barbecue, my preferred style is eastern North Carolina—a whole hog 'cue with an apple cider vinegar sauce. Saying "preferred" is misleading, because it's the only style I'll eat. When it comes to chicken, however, I like chicken with mustard sauce, dry rubbed, smoked, with vinegar sauces, and with sweet ketchup-based sauces. One rule is that I stick to thighs. It takes slightly longer to cook, but the result is worth it—the dark meat is juicy, tender, and full of flavor. Marinated and simmered in barbecue sauce, the thighs take on a new life.

1½ cups ketchup
⅔ cup apple cider vinegar
½ cup water
½ cup packed brown sugar
2 tablespoons mustard
1½ teaspoons cayenne pepper

1 tablespoon garlic powder
1 tablespoon Worcestershire sauce
8 to 10 chicken thighs
2 tablespoons olive oil
Sea salt

1. In a medium bowl, stir together the ketchup, apple cider vinegar, water, brown sugar, mustard, cayenne pepper, garlic powder, and Worcestershire sauce. Transfer half of the sauce to a large resealable plastic bag, add the chicken, seal, and turn to coat. Refrigerate the chicken to marinate in the sauce overnight. Cover and refrigerate the remaining sauce until needed.

2. Preheat the oven to 350°F.

3. Place the skillet over medium-high heat and add the olive oil.

4. Remove the chicken from the sauce, sprinkle with sea salt, and place it in the skillet. Sear for 2 minutes per side.

5. Cover with the reserved barbecue sauce.

6. Move the skillet to the oven and bake for 20 minutes. Flip the chicken and bake for 25 minutes more.

7. Turn the broiler to high, and broil the chicken for 5 minutes before serving.

VARIATION TIP: This is a sweet barbecue sauce with a mild spice. To crank things up a bit, double the cayenne pepper and add a generous pinch of red pepper flakes.

LEMON-ROSEMARY CHICKEN

SERVES 4 / PREP TIME: 20 MINUTES / COOK: 35 MINUTES
CAST IRON: 12-INCH SKILLET

Growing up, this recipe was one of my favorites. In fact, it has been my birthday dinner request for as long as I can remember. The chicken breasts start on the stove top, seared with garlic and rosemary, and are finished in the oven with lemon and butter, leaving them with a crisp skin and a fresh flavor. This year for my birthday, we served it with Garlic Smashed Potatoes (page 71) and arugula salad, making sure to leave room for birthday Blueberry Mountain Pie (page 163).

1 tablespoon olive oil
2 garlic cloves, minced
2 tablespoons fresh rosemary leaves,
     finely chopped

4 boneless skin-on chicken breasts
1 lemon, thinly sliced
Juice of 1 lemon
1 teaspoon sea salt

1. Preheat the oven to 350°F.

2. In the skillet over medium heat, combine the olive oil, garlic, and rosemary. Sauté for 2 to 3 minutes until the garlic browns.

3. Add the chicken to the skillet, searing for 2 minutes per side. Remove the skillet from the heat.

4. Top the chicken with the lemon slices and drizzle the lemon juice over the chicken. Sprinkle with the sea salt.

5. Bake for 30 to 35 minutes until the chicken reaches an internal temperature of 165°F on a meat thermometer.

SERVING TIP: I like to serve this chicken with jasmine rice cooked with butter and topped with a big squeeze of lemon juice.

STUFFED CORNISH HENS
WITH RED POTATOES

SERVES 2 / PREP TIME: 15 MINUTES / COOK TIME: 1 HOUR
CAST IRON: 12-INCH SKILLET

Cornish hens are essentially young chickens. A mix between a Cornish game hen and a White Plymouth Rock hen, they are culled at four to six weeks old and weigh around 2 pounds each. This makes them a wonderful choice for dinner parties and holidays, because a table set with individual birds on each plate, nestled in a bed of red potatoes, makes for an impressive spread. The pork sausage helps keep the birds moist as they roast, adding fat and flavor to the dish. It's certainly a show-stopper to have on hand the next time you have a crowd to impress.

½ pound ground pork sausage
1½ teaspoons red pepper flakes
2 Cornish hens, rinsed well and
    patted dry
¼ cup olive oil
2 garlic cloves, minced
Sea salt

Freshly ground black pepper
½ pound small red potatoes,
    quartered
½ teaspoon ground chipotle
    chile pepper

1. Preheat the oven to 425°F.

2. In a small bowl, mix the sausage and red pepper flakes. Stuff half the sausage into the cavity of each hen.

3. Rub the hens all over with 2 tablespoons of olive oil. Sprinkle each with the garlic, and season with sea salt and black pepper. Place them in the skillet.

4. Arrange the potatoes around the hens. Drizzle the potatoes with the remaining 2 tablespoons of olive oil and season with sea salt and pepper. Sprinkle the chipotle pepper evenly over everything.

5. Roast for 50 to 60 minutes, or until the internal temperature reaches 160°F on a meat thermometer.

VARIATION TIP: Instead of red potatoes, roast the hens with diced butternut squash or fingerling potatoes.

BALSAMIC CHICKEN & MUSHROOMS

SERVES 4 / PREP TIME: 15 MINUTES / COOK TIME: 30 MINUTES
CAST IRON: 12-INCH SKILLET

This dish is comfort food for me—something I save for cold, blustery nights when all I want is to pour a big glass of red wine and curl up next to the fire. The mushrooms cook down and absorb the flavors of the butter and the balsamic vinegar, finishing sweet and tender. I love to make a full skillet and serve it alongside a Pumpkin and Acorn Squash Gratin (page 72) with a nice glass of Malbec.

2 tablespoons olive oil
4 boneless skinless chicken breasts
2 tablespoons salted butter
2 garlic cloves, minced
2 cups porcini mushrooms,
    cleaned and sliced

Sea salt
¼ cup balsamic vinegar
¼ cup chicken broth
5 fresh basil sprigs, minced

1. In the skillet over medium heat, add the olive oil and chicken. Cook for 2 minutes per side. Remove from the skillet and set aside. Return the skillet to medium heat.

2. Add the butter to melt.

3. Stir in the garlic and mushrooms. Cook for 6 to 8 minutes, stirring occasionally, until the mushrooms are softened.

4. Add a pinch of sea salt and stir in the balsamic vinegar and chicken broth.

5. Return the chicken to the skillet and turn twice to coat with the sauce.

6. Reduce the heat to low and cook for 12 to 15 minutes, allowing the liquid to reduce and the chicken to cook through.

7. Remove the skillet from the heat and top the chicken with basil. Serve immediately.

VARIATION TIP: Add a splash of sherry to the sauce for a bit of sweetness.

SPATCHCOCKED CHICKEN

**SERVES 4 / PREP TIME: 30 MINUTES / COOK TIME: 30 MINUTES
CAST IRON: 12-INCH SKILLET**

A spatchcocked chicken is split open to cook quickly. This is accomplished by removing the spine with kitchen scissors and splaying the chicken open in the skillet. Like this, the meat cooks evenly and the skin roasts to that wonderful, crisp golden brown. If you're intimidated by the method, I was, too; I'd expected the process of spatchcocking a bird to be challenging. I'm happy to report that the process is quick and easy, which makes it a fantastic way to roast a chicken.

1 whole chicken, rinsed well
    and patted dry
Sea salt
Freshly ground black pepper
2 garlic cloves, minced

6 fresh sage leaves, minced
1 tablespoon fresh thyme
    leaves, minced
3 tablespoons salted butter,
    at room temperature
Juice of 1 lemon

1. Preheat the oven to 375°F.

2. Lay the chicken flat on a clean work surface, spine up.

3. With the kitchen scissors, starting at the thigh, cut up along one side of the backbone. Repeat on the other side. Completely remove and discard the spine.

4. Flip the chicken on the work surface. Spread it open and flatten it as much as possible. Season the cavity with sea salt and black pepper. Transfer to your skillet, breast-side up.

5. In a small bowl, mix the garlic, sage, and thyme with the butter, crushing the herbs into the butter to release their oils.

6. Rub the chicken with the herb butter, working it under the skin where possible. Season with sea salt and pepper.

7. Roast for 30 minutes, or until the internal temperature reaches 165°F on a meat thermometer and the skin is golden brown and crisp.

8. Sprinkle with the lemon juice and serve.

VARIATION TIP: Don't stop here! Try spatchcocked turkey (cook for 1 hour), quail (cook for 10 minutes), or Cornish hens (cook for 35 minutes)!

GARLIC SPLIT CHICKEN

SERVES 2 TO 4 / PREP TIME: 15 MINUTES / COOK TIME: 30 MINUTES
CAST IRON: 12-INCH SKILLET

I try to stock up when I see meat specials at the grocery store. Keep an eye out for split chicken breasts. Bone-in chicken breasts have the best of both worlds—they are similar in appearance and flavor to a whole chicken, but the work of splitting, cleaning, and deconstructing the chicken has been done for you. So for a small amount of effort, you get fall-off-the-bone tender chicken with thin, crisp skin. And if you keep a few of these in your freezer, you've always got an easy dinner on hand.

2 tablespoons salted butter
6 garlic cloves, minced
2 bone-in, skin-on split chicken breasts,
    patted dry
¼ cup apple cider vinegar

1 tablespoon dried oregano
1 tablespoon dried thyme
1 tablespoon dried
    herbes de Provence
1 teaspoon sea salt

1. Preheat the oven to 350°F.

2. In the skillet over medium heat, combine the butter and garlic.

3. Add the chicken and sear for 1 minute per side. Remove the skillet from the heat.

4. Brush the chicken with the apple cider vinegar and sprinkle with oregano, thyme, herbes de Provence, and sea salt.

5. Roast for 30 minutes, or until the internal temperature reaches 165°F on a meat thermometer.

6. Let rest for 5 minutes before serving.

INGREDIENT TIP: If you are interested in keeping split breasts in the freezer, experiment with marinating them before freezing. I like to rub them down with olive oil and a quick spice blend of sea salt, herbes de Provence, and garlic powder, and freeze them vacuum-sealed or in a resealable freezer bag.

CILANTRO-LIME TURKEY BURGERS

SERVES 4 / PREP TIME: 15 MINUTES / COOK TIME: 15 MINUTES
CAST IRON: 10-INCH SKILLET AND GRIDDLE (OR SECOND SKILLET)

When Dan and I first graduated from college we excitedly dove into recipe planning, experimenting with different styles of food, ingredients, and cooking methods. One of our favorite meals that ended up in *very* heavy rotation was these turkey burgers—made with a lot of lime juice, minced cilantro, and served with Gruyère cheese. The ginger and cilantro bring a punch of flavor often missing in turkey burgers, and the lime juice helps them stay moist and juicy. Over the years we've played with the recipe but ultimately we come back to this version, agreeing it is as tasty today as it was when we first fell in love with it.

1 pound ground turkey
¼ cup minced fresh cilantro leaves, plus more for serving
1 jalapeño pepper, minced
1 garlic clove, minced
1 teaspoon minced peeled fresh ginger
Pinch sea salt

¼ cup plus 1 tablespoon olive oil, divided
4 buns
Juice of 1 lime
¼ cup shredded Gruyère cheese
Handful dandelion greens

1. In a medium bowl, mix the turkey, cilantro, jalapeño pepper, garlic, ginger, and sea salt. Shape the turkey mixture into 4 patties.

2. In the skillet over medium heat, heat ¼ cup of olive oil.

3. Add the turkey patties and cook for 5 to 6 minutes per side. Remove the cooked burgers to a plate.

4. Preheat the griddle over medium heat.

5. While the burgers cook, brush the cut-side of the buns with the remaining 1 tablespoon of olive oil, and toast on the griddle for 1 to 2 minutes.

6. Sprinkle the lime juice over the cooked burgers. Assemble the burgers on the buns, topping each with the Gruyère, cilantro, and dandelion greens.

PREPARATION TIP: Turkey burgers are easy to overcook—they dry out quickly. Stay close while they're cooking, and eat them while they're hot and juicy!

TURKEY SOUP

SERVES 6 TO 8 / PREP TIME: 30 MINUTES / COOK TIME: 9 HOURS
CAST IRON: DUTCH OVEN

One of the best things about cooking a whole turkey is that after the feast, you have the base for delicious turkey soup. I start by making the stock: Simmer the carcass, skin, and odds and ends in water with vegetables, herbs, and spices. This leaves you with a rich, delicious stock ready for leftover turkey and final vegetables. The flavor builds as the soup simmers on the stove for an afternoon, coming together slowly and simply. It's the perfect recipe for a day spent around the house, with pockets of time to stop by the kitchen, stirring here and there, tasting, adjusting spices, and adding ingredients.

FOR THE STOCK
1 turkey carcass/remains
2 carrots
1 onion
1 whole garlic head
1 tablespoon red pepper flakes
1 tablespoon sea salt

FOR THE SOUP
4 cups cooked shredded turkey meat
5 red potatoes, chopped
2 carrots, chopped
2 purple beets, peeled and chopped
2 golden beets, peeled and chopped
1 white onion, chopped
3 garlic cloves, chopped
Sea salt
Freshly ground black pepper
Cooked rice, warmed, for serving

1. In the Dutch oven over high heat, combine the turkey carcass, carrots, onion, garlic, red pepper flakes, and sea salt. Cover with water and bring to a boil. Reduce the heat to low and simmer for 6 hours, stirring occasionally.

2. Strain the stock, discard the turkey carcass and vegetables, and return the stock to the pot.

TO MAKE THE SOUP

1. Add the turkey, potatoes, carrots, purple beets, golden beets, onion, and garlic to the pot. Simmer for 3 hours, stirring and adjusting the seasoning as it cooks.

2. Serve over rice.

INGREDIENT TIP: When you cook the turkey, freeze the gizzards and neck. When you're ready to make the stock, add them to the mix.

BOURBON QUAIL

SERVES 4 / PREP TIME: 30 MINUTES / COOK TIME: 2 HOURS, 20 MINUTES
CAST IRON: 12-INCH SKILLET AND 10-INCH SKILLET

I was a touch terrified the first time I cooked quail. They're just so *little*. I quickly overcame my fear when I realized that despite the size, quail requires the same skills needed to cook any poultry effectively. I have come to love the bird, and have tried it stuffed, roasted, fried, and grilled. My husband's favorite take is quail suffused in a thick bourbon barbecue sauce. Rich and sweet with a touch of spice, the sauce complements the delicate flavor of the quail, particularly when served with risotto or a big pot of Gouda grits (see page 101).

1 tablespoon salted butter
1 shallot, minced
2 garlic cloves, minced
¼ cup tomato paste
3 cups water
½ cup bourbon

2 tablespoons ketchup
1 tablespoon whole-grain mustard
1 teaspoon garlic powder
1 teaspoon sea salt
1 teaspoon hot sauce
8 quail

1. In the 12-inch skillet over medium heat, melt the butter.

2. Add the shallot and garlic and stir in the tomato paste. Cook for 3 to 4 minutes, stirring frequently, until the shallot browns and the tomato paste has caramelized.

3. Whisk in the water, bourbon, ketchup, mustard, garlic powder, sea salt, and hot sauce. Reduce the heat to low, cover the skillet, and simmer for 2 hours, stirring occasionally. Set aside half of the sauce.

4. Preheat the oven to 350°F.

5. In the 10-inch skillet over medium-high heat, sear each quail for 1 minute per side. Place the quail into the 12-inch skillet, and coat each with bourbon sauce.

6. Roast for 12 to 15 minutes until the quails' internal temperature reaches 140°F on a meat thermometer. Top with the reserved sauce and serve.

SERVING TIP: Serve with your favorite bourbon drink and enjoy!

SEARED DUCK BREAST
WITH APPLE CIDER

SERVES 2 / PREP TIME: 20 MINUTES / COOK TIME: 20 MINUTES
CAST IRON: 10-INCH SKILLET

You hear duck fat talked about with tones of awe for good reason—it is delicious, and everything it touches gets more delicious. If you've never had duck fat fries, trust me on this one. Seared duck breast takes full advantage of this, slowly rendering its fat to cook the breast so the skin has the crunch you hope for while the meat cooks to an ideal medium-rare.

½ cup apple cider
2 tablespoons honey
2 garlic cloves, minced
1 tablespoon whole allspice berries
1 tablespoon apple cider vinegar

2 skin-on duck breasts, scored in a crosshatch pattern piercing the fat layer
Sea salt
Freshly ground black pepper

1. In a small pot over medium heat, combine ½ cup of apple cider, the honey, garlic, and allspice. Simmer for about 15 minutes to reduce, stirring frequently. Strain out the allspice berries before serving.

2. Brush the duck breasts with 1 tablespoon of cider vinegar and season with sea salt and black pepper.

3. Place the duck skin-side down in a cold skillet. Place the skillet over medium heat and cook for 6 to 8 minutes, allowing the duck fat to slowly render and the skin to crisp.

4. Flip the duck and cook for 5 minutes, or until the internal temperature reaches 125°F to 130°F on a meat thermometer.

5. Let the duck rest for 5 minutes. Slice and drizzle with the cider-honey.

INGREDIENT TIP: Duck fat is a delicious addition to many dishes. Reserve the fat and use it instead of butter when you make Pan-Seared Steak (page 146) or roasted potatoes.

CHAPTER 7

MEAT

SAUSAGE, POTATO & KALE SOUP

SERVES 6 / PREP TIME: 25 MINUTES / COOK TIME: 2 HOURS, 45 MINUTES
CAST IRON: DUTCH OVEN

When I think of winter, this soup immediately comes to mind. It is the epitome of hearty, with a rich creamy broth that fills you up and warms you body and soul. This also is, in my opinion, the perfect recipe for a Dutch oven. Building a soup from the beginning allows you to layer the flavor, and the result is more complex because of it. This soup begins with tasty pork sausage; the spices, flavor, and fat blend as it simmers and comes together.

1 tablespoon salted butter
1 pound chorizo fresco or
   spicy Italian sausage
2 garlic cloves, minced
1 large white onion or
   yellow onion, chopped
10 to 12 small red potatoes or
   mixed-color potatoes, quartered

8 cups chicken broth
Sea salt
Freshly ground black pepper
Pinch red pepper flakes
1 bunch kale, stemmed and chopped
2 cups heavy (whipping) cream

1. In the Dutch oven over medium heat, melt the butter.

2. Add the chorizo, garlic, and onion. Cook for 5 to 7 minutes, stirring frequently, until the chorizo is cooked and the garlic and onion soften.

3. Stir in the potatoes. Cook, stirring often, for 5 minutes, until browned.

4. Add the chicken broth, a dash of sea salt and black pepper, and the red pepper flakes. Bring to a boil. Reduce the heat to medium-low, cover, and simmer for 2 hours, stirring frequently. Taste and adjust the seasoning as needed.

5. Stir in the kale and heavy cream. Simmer for 30 minutes, covered, until the potatoes are soft.

6. Season with sea salt and black pepper as needed. Serve hot.

   INGREDIENT TIP: Use any bitter green, such as collards or chard.

SAUSAGE with SWEET POTATO & LEEKS

SERVES 2 / PREP TIME: 10 MINUTES / COOK TIME: 15 MINUTES
CAST IRON: 12-INCH SKILLET

Our family's dinner dish of the moment is a quick skillet bowl of sausage, sweet potato, and leeks. Leeks are wonderful because their flavor is reminiscent of their allium cousins, garlic and onion. The combination of the three flavors—the spice of the sausage, the sweetness of the sweet potato, and the crunch and freshness of the leeks—creates a dish that is filling and satisfying, one that Dan and I eagerly add to the menu each week.

2 chorizo fresco or
   spicy Italian sausage
1 tablespoon olive oil
1 sweet potato, peeled and
   diced into ½-inch cubes
1 garlic clove, minced

1 leek, (white and light green parts)
   rinsed well and thinly sliced
Pinch sea salt
Pinch red pepper flakes
½ pound mozzarella

1. In the skillet over medium heat, cook the chorizo fresco for 5 minutes per side. Remove from the skillet and set aside.

2. Return the skillet to medium heat. Add the olive oil, sweet potato, and garlic. Cook for 5 to 7 minutes, stirring frequently, until the sweet potato begins to soften.

3. Add the leek, sea salt, and red pepper flakes.

4. Slice the cooled sausage and return it to the skillet. Stir well and cook for 3 to 5 minutes until the leek browns.

5. Remove from the heat, and top with the mozzarella to serve.

PREPARATION TIP: Leeks can collect a lot of dirt in the sheath. When you clean them, rinse well between the layers down toward the root.

DUTCH OVEN BRUNSWICK STEW

SERVES 6 TO 8 / PREP TIME: 1 HOUR / COOK TIME: 8 HOURS, 45 MINUTES
CAST IRON: DUTCH OVEN

Brunswick stew has deep historical roots in the south and is still popular from Virginia to Georgia. It is traditionally made in huge batches in giant cast iron laundry cauldrons. While this tradition is valuable (see page 12), I've worked to make a Dutch oven adaptation that is more manageable for the average home cook. And when I say "worked," I truly mean it. It was *hard* to come up with a Brunswick stew that could be made indoors, in less than 24 hours, and still have a flavor true to the original. Of all the recipes in this book, this is the one I'm the most proud of; it's perhaps the biggest culinary feat I've pulled off. Have I talked it up enough yet? Trust me, it's worth the effort.

1 whole chicken, cleaned
Sea salt
Freshly ground black pepper
1 tablespoon salted butter
One 1.6-pound bone-in pork loin end
2 tablespoons olive oil
24 fingerling potatoes, chopped
3 celery stalks with
    tender greens, chopped

1 white onion, chopped
3 garlic cloves, minced
Two 15-ounce cans butter beans,
    rinsed and drained
Two 15-ounce cans corn, drained
Two 28-ounce cans diced tomatoes,
    with the juice
1 cup water
3 tablespoons Worcestershire sauce
2 teaspoons red pepper flakes

1. To the Dutch oven over medium-low heat, add the chicken, enough water to cover, and a pinch of sea salt and black pepper. Cover and cook for 4 hours. Transfer the chicken and cooking liquid to a large bowl.

2. Preheat the oven to 300°F.

3. Put the Dutch oven over medium heat and add the butter to melt.

4. Add the pork and brown it for 30 seconds per side. Remove from the pot and set aside.

5. Return the pot to medium heat. Add the olive oil, potatoes, celery, onion, and garlic. Cook for 10 to 12 minutes, stirring frequently, until the onion begins to brown.

6. Stir in the butter beans, corn, tomatoes, and water. Return the pork to the pot and reduce the heat to low.

7. Stir in the Worcestershire sauce and red pepper flakes. Season with sea salt and pepper. Simmer for 30 minutes.

8. Return the chicken and cooking liquid to the pot. Stir well. Cover the pot and carefully transfer it to the oven. Cook for 4 hours, checking the seasoning every hour and giving it a good bottom-scraping stir, breaking up the pork as it cooks.

9. Season with sea salt and black pepper as needed. Serve hot.

PREPARATION TIP: Instead of transferring the Dutch oven to the oven to continue cooking, try transferring it to a smoker following the recipe as is!

CAULDRON BRUNSWICK STEW

SERVES 20 TO 25 / PREP TIME: 3 DAYS / COOK TIME: 8 HOURS
CAST IRON: 40-QUART CAULDRON

Every year or two, my father invests the better part of a week in a time-honored family tradition: making Brunswick stew. This stew, a traditional Southern catch-all, combines a medley of vegetables and whatever game meat you have on hand. He makes the stew in his grandmother's cauldron, and the recipe we work from is hers. Sybil's recipe makes 40 quarts of stew, and takes three days to pull together. It is a labor of love, but it is more than just stew—it's family, tradition, and nourishment. It's the kind of food that crosses generations and helps keep Southern food culture alive and present. Plus, it's damn tasty.

FOR DAY 1
6 whole chickens and innards,
    chickens quartered
Sea salt
Two 10- to 12½-pound bone-in
    pork shoulders

FOR DAY 2
25 pounds potatoes, peeled
2 pounds dried butter beans
Sea salt

FOR DAY 3
5 pounds white or
    yellow onions, chopped
2 quarts canned green butter beans,
    rinsed and drained

6 quarts canned corn, drained
1 whole garlic head, minced
½ cup sea salt, plus more as needed
½ cup freshly ground black pepper,
    plus more as needed
¼ cup garlic powder,
    plus more as needed
2 tablespoons chili powder,
    plus more as needed
15 ounces Worcestershire sauce
12 ounces hot sauce (my father
    recommends Texas Pete)
4 gallons whole peeled tomatoes
    or diced tomatoes with the juice
Eight 15-ounce cans tomato purée
1 bottle red wine, such as merlot

ON DAY 1

1. In large pots over high heat, combine the chicken, innards, enough water to cover, and 1 tablespoon of sea salt per pot. Boil for about 45 minutes until the chicken is cooked through.

2. Remove the chicken, shred the meat, place in a 5-gallon container with a lid, and set aside.

3. Return the water to a boil. Add the pork and cook for 1 hour, or until the meat is falling off the bone. Remove the pork, shred the meat, mix with the chicken in the 5-gallon container, and pour in the cooking liquid. Cover and refrigerate.

ON DAY 2

1. In a 5-gallon container, combine the potatoes with enough water to cover, and let soak.

2. In a large pot, combine the dried butter beans, 2 tablespoons of sea salt, enough water to cover, and let soak.

ON DAY 3

1. Place the cauldron on a propane burner set up outside. Turn the heat to high.

2. Drain the potatoes, quarter them, and add them to the cauldron along with enough fresh water to cover.

3. Drain the soaking butter beans and add them to the pot. Add more water, if needed, to cover.

4. Stir in the onions and green butter beans. Cook for 40 to 45 minutes, stirring frequently so nothing sticks to the bottom. (We recommend a paddle for stirring. A clean wooden hockey stick works, too!)

5. Remove the pot with the chicken and pork from the refrigerator and scoop off and discard the fat. Stir the shredded meat and cooking liquid into the cauldron. Bring the stew to a boil.

6. Add the corn and garlic. Stir well to combine.

7. Add the sea salt, black pepper, garlic powder, chili powder, Worcestershire sauce, and hot sauce.

8. Cook, uncovered, for about 3 hours, keeping the heat at about medium-high. It will not be boiling but should be hot. Stir frequently.

9. When the beans are soft, stir in the tomatoes, tomato purée, and red wine. Cook for 2 hours, stirring frequently.

10. Adjust the seasoning. Serve hot, ladled into bowls.

11. Portion any leftovers into resealable containers and distribute these highly prized souvenirs to friends and family.

SERVING TIP: Serve with a big heaping hunk of Skillet Corn Bread (page 50) on the side.

PORK PORTERHOUSE

SERVES 2 / PREP TIME: 5 MINUTES / COOK TIME: 15 MINUTES
CAST IRON: 10-INCH SKILLET

A pork porterhouse, also known as a pork chop, is a tender cut of pork loin. When served bone-in and cooked quickly over high heat, it has the potential to be moist and flavorful. More so than steak, pork has a tendency to dry out rapidly if over-cooked, so it's important to be attentive while you're cooking. The recommended internal temperatures for cooked pork have shifted over the years, but in general, serving a medium chop with an internal temperature between 140°F and 150°F is both safe and delicious.

2 bone-in pork porterhouse steaks, patted dry
1 teaspoon sea salt
½ teaspoon freshly ground black pepper

1 tablespoon olive oil
1 tablespoon salted butter
½ teaspoon red pepper flakes
½ teaspoon ground paprika

1. Season both sides of the pork with the sea salt and black pepper.

2. In the skillet over medium-high heat, combine the olive oil and butter.

3. Add the pork and cook for 3 to 4 minutes per side until golden brown. On a meat thermometer, the internal temperature should reach between 140°F and 150°F for medium, and 160°F for well done.

4. Let the pork rest for 5 minutes before serving.

PREPARATION TIP: It's also important to let the pork (and all meats) rest for at least 5 minutes before serving to allow the juices to redistribute.

PORK TENDERLOIN WITH APPLES & ROOT VEGETABLES

SERVES 4 / PREP TIME: 25 MINUTES / COOK TIME: 1 HOUR
CAST IRON: 12-INCH SKILLET

The beauty of pork tenderloin comes in its versatility, its ease of preparation, and the fact that it is a relatively healthy cut of meat. Pork tenderloin lends itself to many flavors and cooking techniques, from roasted to slow cooked. In the fall and early winter, I love to roast it on a bed of root vegetables and sliced apples, filling my house with the sweet scent of beets and rosemary.

2 carrots, roughly chopped

2 red potatoes, roughly chopped

1 white onion, roughly chopped

1 golden beet, peeled and roughly chopped

1 purple beet, peeled and roughly chopped

1 large apple, roughly chopped

2 garlic cloves, minced, divided

1 tablespoon fresh rosemary leaves, divided

1 tablespoon fresh oregano leaves, divided

1 tablespoon fresh thyme leaves, divided

2 tablespoons olive oil

2 pounds pork tenderloin

2 tablespoons apple cider vinegar

Sea salt

Freshly ground black pepper

1. Preheat the oven to 350°F.

2. In the skillet, toss together the carrots, potatoes, onion, golden beet, purple beet, apple, half of the garlic, 1½ teaspoons of rosemary, 1½ teaspoons of oregano, and 1½ teaspoons of thyme. Coat the vegetables with the olive oil and spread them in the skillet.

3. Baste the pork with the apple cider vinegar, the remaining garlic, and the remaining 1½ teaspoons of rosemary, 1½ teaspoons of oregano, and 1½ teaspoons of thyme. Nestle the pork into the vegetables.

4. Roast for 1 hour, or until the internal temperature reaches 160°F on a meat thermometer.

5. Let rest for 5 minutes before serving.

SERVING TIP: Leftover pork slices make delicious sandwiches. Try it on toasted slices of No-Knead Dutch Oven Bread (page 61).

GUMBO

SERVES 6 / PREP TIME: 20 MINUTES / COOK TIME: 2 HOURS
CAST IRON: DUTCH OVEN

A few years ago I had the great pleasure of traveling to Avery Island, Louisiana, to spend a week with the McIlhenny family and learn about Cajun and Creole cuisines, and how their hot sauce, Tabasco, is woven into it. It was an incredible week, and we ate and drank so well that I still think about it often. One of the most memorable meals we had was a double gumbo feast, where New Orleans chef Sue Zemanick and Avery Island's chef, Nelson Boutte, sparred with dueling gumbos. Chef Zemanick prepared a vegetarian gumbo *des herbes* topped with a deviled quail egg, while Chef Boutte prepared a more traditional meat and seafood gumbo. Both were incredibly delicious, and I learned more about roux in one afternoon than I thought possible (see Preparation Tip).

½ pound thick-cut bacon
4 andouille sausages
1 boneless skinless chicken breast
½ cup (1 stick) salted butter
3 celery stalks with tender
    greens, chopped
1 green bell pepper,
    seeded and chopped
1 white onion, chopped
2 garlic cloves, chopped
1 cup all-purpose flour
2 tablespoons ground paprika
1 tablespoon gumbo filé powder
1 teaspoon dried oregano

1 teaspoon ground coriander
1 teaspoon ground cumin
1 teaspoon dried thyme
1 teaspoon cayenne pepper
1 teaspoon red pepper flakes
6 cups chicken broth
12 okra, thinly sliced
1 jalapeño pepper, minced
1 teaspoon sea salt
One 5-ounce bottle hot sauce
2 pounds shrimp, peeled and deveined
6 eggs
6 to 8 cups cooked rice

1. In the Dutch oven over medium heat, fry the bacon for 5 to 6 minutes. With a slotted spoon, remove the bacon, leaving the grease in the pot, and set it aside.

2. Add the sausages to the pot, and cook for 8 to 10 minutes, turning occasionally, until done. Remove from the pot and set aside.

3. Add the chicken to the pot. Cook for 5 minutes per side. Remove from the pot and set aside.

4. Stir the butter into the bacon drippings.

5. Stir in the celery, bell pepper, and onion. Cook for 3 to 4 minutes, until the onion begins to brown.

6. Whisk in the garlic, flour, paprika, gumbo filé powder, oregano, coriander, cumin, thyme, cayenne pepper, and red pepper flakes. Cook for 5 minutes, whisking constantly until the roux browns.

7. While continuing to whisk, slowly pour in the chicken broth. Simmer for 20 minutes.

8. Shred the chicken and slice the sausage. Return them to the pot.

9. Stir in the okra and jalapeño pepper.

10. Add the sea salt and hot sauce, and stir. Simmer for 1 hour more.

11. Stir in the shrimp. Cook for 4 to 5 minutes until they are opaque.

12. In a medium pot of salted boiling water over high heat, boil the eggs for 6 minutes. Let cool and peel (they will be soft-boiled).

13. In a large soup bowl, serve a generous portion of gumbo over 1 cup of warm rice. Top with an egg and some crumbled bacon.

PREPARATION TIP: The biggest trick I learned about working with roux is to melt the butter until it becomes bubbly, stirring constantly with a wooden spoon as you add the flour a little at a time. Once the roux darkens, continue to stir constantly as you add the liquid.

SERVING TIP: Try this gumbo topped with deviled eggs (or, better yet, deviled quail eggs).

DUTCH OVEN PULLED PORK

SERVES 4 TO 6 / PREP TIME: 5 MINUTES / COOK TIME: 6 HOURS
CAST IRON: DUTCH OVEN

I am particular about pulled pork barbecue. It is deserving of the title "barbecue" only when slow cooked over an open flame, sauced with apple cider vinegar, salt, and red pepper, and served with cole slaw and hush puppies. That said, this recipe is *not* barbecue. It is, however, slow-cooked pulled pork made in the Dutch oven and sauced in the style of eastern North Carolina barbecue. If you don't have an open pit of coals and a whole hog handy, this is a pretty darn good imitation. The trick with both traditional barbecue and Dutch oven pulled pork is time—and the waiting is a bit easier with a batch of Spicy Boiled Peanuts (page 70) to snack on.

One 5-pound bone-in pork shoulder
2 cups apple cider vinegar
1 tablespoon liquid smoke

1 tablespoon red pepper flakes
1 tablespoon sea salt

1. Preheat the oven to 275°F.

2. Place the pork in the Dutch oven, fat-side up.

3. Pour the apple cider vinegar and liquid smoke over the pork.

4. Sprinkle with the red pepper flakes and sea salt.

5. Cover and cook for 6 hours, occasionally basting with the liquid.

6. Shred the pork and mix well with the juices before serving.

SERVING TIP: Our family loves to serve our pulled pork with kimchi and a squeeze of fresh lime.

RED WINE-BRAISED SHORT RIBS

SERVES 2 / PREP TIME: 10 MINUTES / INACTIVE TIME: 12 HOURS
COOK TIME: 3 HOURS, 30 MINUTES
CAST IRON: DUTCH OVEN

This dish is part of my collection of go-to dinner party dishes. Braising short ribs in red wine and broth cooks them slowly, rendering them so tender they fall off the bone. After the first bite, you put down your fork, close your eyes, and savor, exactly the experience I'm trying to cultivate.

6 beef short ribs

1 bottle red wine, such as cabernet or merlot, divided

1 tablespoon black peppercorns, divided

1 tablespoon fresh rosemary leaves, divided

1 teaspoon dried oregano, divided

1 dried bay leaf, divided

8 tablespoons (1 stick) salted butter, divided

Sea salt

Freshly ground black pepper

6 cups beef broth

1. The night before, in a large resealable plastic bag, combine the ribs, half of the bottle of wine, 1½ teaspoons of peppercorns, 1½ teaspoons of rosemary, ½ teaspoon of oregano, and ½ of bay leaf. Seal the bag, turn to coat, and refrigerate overnight to marinate.

2. Preheat the oven to 375°F.

3. In the Dutch oven over medium-high heat, melt 4 tablespoons of butter.

4. Remove the ribs from the marinade, wipe off the peppercorns, pat dry, and put in the pot. Season with sea salt and black pepper. Cook for 1 to 2 minutes per side to brown.

5. Cover with the remaining wine and the beef broth. Add the remaining 4 tablespoons of butter, 1½ teaspoons of peppercorns, 1½ teaspoons of rosemary, ½ teaspoon of oregano, and ½ of bay leaf. Stir to combine.

6. Cover, transfer to the oven, and braise for 3½ hours. Remove the peppercorns and bay leaf before serving.

SERVING TIP: Serve on a bed of creamy Gouda grits (see page 101) topped with scallions.

PAN-SEARED STEAK

SERVES 1 TO 2 / PREP TIME: 5 MINUTES / COOK TIME: 10 TO 15 MINUTES
CAST IRON: 10-INCH SKILLET

Once or twice a month I like to indulge in a really nice steak. When pan-seared just right in hot butter with a little bit of garlic, and served with an arugula salad and Garlic Smashed Potatoes (page 71), this steak feels extravagant. It makes a superb home-cooked dinner for date night, especially if you pour yourself a glass of wine while you cook. This is an instance when high-quality ingredients matter, because what will shine through is the quality of the steak. I use tenderloins or strip steaks because they are tender, somewhat fatty, and full of flavor. Strip steaks also stand up well to high heat, which allows for a beautiful sear on the outside. When you've got a nice steak and a well-seasoned skillet, who needs a steakhouse?

1 pound beef strip steak, 1 inch thick, at room temperature, patted dry

1 teaspoon kosher salt

½ teaspoon freshly ground black pepper

3 tablespoons salted butter, divided

1 garlic clove, minced

1. Sprinkle each side of the steak with the kosher salt and black pepper.

2. In the skillet over medium-high heat, melt 2 tablespoons of butter.

3. Add the garlic to the skillet. Cook for about 1 minute, stirring frequently, until it begins to brown.

4. Add the steak. Cook for 5 minutes and flip. Continue cooking. For a rare steak: Cook for 3 to 5 minutes more, or until the internal temperature reaches 135°F on a meat thermometer. For a medium steak: Cook for 5 to 7 minutes more, or until the internal temperature reaches 140°F. For a medium-well steak: Cook for 8 to 10 minutes more, or until the internal temperature reaches 150°F.

5. Transfer to a warmed dinner plate and let rest for 5 minutes.

6. Top with the remaining 1 tablespoon of butter and serve.

VARIATION TIP: In a food processor (or blender), cream together 4 tablespoons (½ stick) of salted room-temperature butter with 1 tablespoon of chopped fresh herbs such as rosemary, basil, or sage, and top the steak with your favorite herbed butter!

SHEPHERD'S PIE

SERVES 4 / PREP TIME: 45 MINUTES / COOK TIME: 45 MINUTES
CAST IRON: 12-INCH SKILLET

Shepherd's pie, also known as cottage pie, is a mixture of peas, carrots, corn, onion, and ground beef topped with a thick layer of creamy mashed potatoes. Baked all together and served so you get a little bit of everything, it's a dish that is simple to make but leaves an impression. Clearly, since I still remember the shepherd pie our neighbors, the Nearys, used to make when I was growing up!

2 Yukon gold potatoes, quartered

7 tablespoons salted butter, divided

¾ cup mayonnaise

Sea salt

Freshly ground black pepper

1 pound 85% lean ground beef

2 carrots, chopped

1 cup frozen peas

1 white onion, chopped

½ cup corn kernels, drained

2 garlic cloves, minced

1 teaspoon red pepper flakes

1 teaspoon Worcestershire sauce

1. In a medium saucepan over high heat, boil the potatoes for about 20 minutes until soft. Drain and transfer to a large bowl.

2. Add 6 tablespoons of butter, the mayonnaise, and a pinch of sea salt and pepper. With a handheld mixer, mix at medium speed until the potatoes are mashed and combined. Alternatively, you can use a potato masher. Set aside.

3. In the skillet over medium heat, melt the remaining 1 tablespoon of butter.

4. Add the ground beef and cook for 8 to 10 minutes until cooked through and browned.

5. Stir in the carrots, peas, onion, corn, garlic, red pepper flakes, and Worcestershire sauce. Cook for 15 minutes, stirring frequently.

6. Preheat the oven to 350°F.

7. Spoon the mashed potatoes over the filling in the skillet. Transfer to the oven and bake for 45 minutes. Serve hot.

VARIATION TIP: Top with 1 cup of grated white Cheddar cheese before baking.

LONDON BROIL WITH CHIMICHURRI SAUCE

SERVES 4 / PREP TIME: 10 MINUTES / COOK TIME: 15 MINUTES
CAST IRON: 12-INCH SKILLET

I always thought that a "London broil" sounded so elegant. My grandmother Barbara, who came of age as a home cook when London broils were very much in vogue, saved the dish for dinner parties and special events. When I came of age as a home cook and started experimenting with different meats, I was surprised to learn that, when prepared properly, London broils are about as easy as beef gets. In fact, in the Venn diagram of steak that is affordable and steak that is delicious, London broil falls squarely in the middle. The trick with London broil is that it needs a good sear and to be cooked, nay *broiled*, under very high temperatures. This makes cast iron the ideal tool, since the skillet, preheated with the oven to 500°F, can easily withstand the temperature and deliver a beautiful sear. While my grandmother served London broil with lemon, I prefer to finish mine with chimichurri, an Argentinian sauce made with parsley, garlic, and vinegar.

FOR THE CHIMICHURRI

1 cup fresh parsley leaves
½ cup fresh cilantro leaves
⅓ cup red wine vinegar
3 garlic cloves
1 teaspoon red pepper flakes
½ teaspoon sea salt
½ cup olive oil

FOR THE STEAK

2 pounds London broil steak, patted dry
2 tablespoons olive oil
1 teaspoon sea salt
1 teaspoon freshly ground black pepper

TO MAKE THE CHIMICHURRI

In a food processor (or blender), blend the parsley, cilantro, red wine vinegar, garlic, red pepper flakes, and sea salt. While continuing to blend, add the olive oil in a thin steady stream, to cause the sauce to become an emulsion. Pour into a lidded jar and set aside.

TO MAKE THE STEAK

1. Preheat the oven broiler to high.

2. Place the dry skillet on the middle oven rack to heat for 10 minutes.

3. Rub the steak on both sides with the olive oil, sea salt, and black pepper.

4. After 10 minutes, place the meat in the skillet. Broil for 6 minutes, flip, and broil for 6 minutes. For a rare finish, cook for 5 minutes per side; for medium-well, cook for 7 minutes per side.

5. Remove from the heat and let rest for 5 minutes.

6. Slice the steak, shake the chimichurri sauce, and pour over the steak.

VARIATION TIP: On weeknights, we like to serve this London broil over a spinach salad with feta cheese, sliced red onions, and cucumbers. The chimichurri sauce makes a great salad dressing.

MEATLOAF

SERVES 4 TO 6 / PREP TIME: 10 MINUTES / COOK TIME: 1 HOUR
CAST IRON: BISCUIT PAN

My friend Aaron tested many recipes in this book, and his reaction to this meat-loaf was, "Wow, was this moist and delicious. It's the best meatloaf I've ever had. The next morning I crumbled some in the cast iron skillet for those delicious crispy bits, and added an egg for a breakfast treat." So there you have it, straight from the recipe tester's mouth, with a bonus suggestion for how to treat leftovers.

FOR THE SAUCE
½ cup apple cider vinegar
3 tablespoons packed brown sugar
½ cup tomato paste

FOR THE MEATLOAF
2 pounds 85% lean ground beef
1 cup bread crumbs
½ cup tomato paste
½ cup whole milk

4 garlic cloves, minced
2 eggs, lightly beaten
1 white onion, finely chopped
1 teaspoon sea salt
1 teaspoon garlic powder
1 teaspoon ground paprika
1 teaspoon dry mustard
½ teaspoon cayenne pepper

TO MAKE THE SAUCE

In a small bowl, stir together the apple cider vinegar, brown sugar, and tomato paste. Set aside.

TO MAKE THE MEATLOAF

1. Preheat the oven to 350°F.

2. In a large bowl, mix the ground beef, bread crumbs, tomato paste, milk, garlic, eggs, onion, sea salt, garlic powder, paprika, dry mustard, and cayenne pepper. Divide the meat mixture evenly among the wells of your biscuit pan.

3. Spread half the sauce over the meatloaves.

4. Bake the meatloaf for 1 hour, with the biscuit pan placed atop a baking pan to catch any leaks. Top with the remaining sauce and serve.

SERVING TIP: Serve with mashed potatoes. Meatloaf should *always* be served with mashed potatoes.

BURGERS

SERVES 4 / PREP TIME: 15 MINUTES / COOK TIME: 10 MINUTES
CAST IRON: 10-INCH SKILLET AND GRIDDLE

When I was pregnant, I craved well-made hamburgers, and it fell on my husband to facilitate my cravings. His go-to method includes a clove of minced garlic, Worcestershire sauce, and feta cheese mixed in with the burger. I also swear by 85% lean ground beef (because a bit more fat in the blend means more flavor), and Duke's mayonnaise. Duke's has a cult following in the South for good reason—it's delicious and sets itself apart from other mayonnaise recipes because it has no added sugar. Serve the burgers on buttered, toasted buns, and there's basically no need to go out for burgers again.

1 pound 85% lean ground beef
½ cup feta cheese
1 tablespoon Worcestershire sauce
1 garlic clove, minced
1 teaspoon sea salt
1 or 2 dashes hot sauce

4 hamburger buns
2 tablespoons salted butter, divided
¼ red onion, thinly sliced
Handful arugula
¼ cup mayonnaise
 (Duke's if you can find it)

1. In a large bowl, mix the ground beef, feta cheese, Worcestershire sauce, garlic, sea salt, and hot sauce. Divide the meat mixture into 4 patties and shape them into ½-inch-thick rounds.

2. In the skillet over medium heat, melt 1 tablespoon of butter.

3. Add the burgers and cook for 5 minutes per side for medium-rare or 6 minutes per side for medium.

4. While the burgers cook, place the griddle over medium-high heat, butter the buns with the remaining 1 tablespoon of butter, and toast them on the griddle for about 2 minutes.

5. Top the burgers with the sliced onion, some arugula, a dollop of the mayonnaise, and serve.

SERVING TIP: During the fall, I love to make quick pickled tomatoes by simmering sliced green tomatoes (½ inch thick) with apple cider vinegar (enough to cover the tomatoes halfway). These make a fantastic topping for any burger.

CHICKEN FRIED STEAK WITH ROSEMARY GRAVY

SERVES 4 / PREP TIME: 20 MINUTES / COOK TIME: 15 MINUTES
CAST IRON: 10-INCH SKILLET

When I was in seventh grade, I read Upton Sinclair's *The Jungle* and promptly became a vegetarian. The Sunday after I made this life-changing decision, we headed to my grandmother's house for dinner. She had made chicken fried steak with jasmine rice and a thick pepper gravy, and I knew I had to break the news to her gently. I took a deep breath and said, "Bobbie, I've decided I'm a vegetarian now; I'm not eating meat anymore." She looked at me with a very measured face and said, "Well that's fine, honey, you can just eat rice and gravy." She loaded me up a big plate of rice topped with fried steak gravy and smiled at me. I didn't have the heart to point out that the gravy was really quite full of meat, so my first Sunday supper as a vegetarian was decidedly *not* vegetarian. Many years later, I found myself living far away from home and really missing her. I wasn't a vegetarian anymore, so I made her chicken fried steak and told this story to my husband, Dan, which turned out to be the perfect cure for homesickness.

2 cups all-purpose flour, divided

1 tablespoon garlic powder, divided

1 teaspoon sea salt, divided, plus more as needed

1 teaspoon cayenne pepper, divided

1 teaspoon ground paprika, divided

2 eggs

1 tablespoon apple cider vinegar

1 tablespoon hot sauce

1 cup bread crumbs

4 beef cubed steaks, pounded to ¼ inch thick

Peanut oil or coconut oil, for frying

1¼ cups chicken broth

½ cup heavy (whipping) cream

1 tablespoon chopped fresh rosemary leaves

1 teaspoon freshly ground black pepper

1. On a clean work surface, line up 3 small bowls. In the first bowl, mix 1 cup of flour, 1½ teaspoons of garlic powder, ½ teaspoon of sea salt, ½ teaspoon of cayenne pepper, and ½ teaspoon of paprika. In the second bowl, whisk together the eggs, apple cider vinegar, and hot sauce. In the third bowl, mix the remaining 1 cup of flour, the bread crumbs, and the remaining 1½ teaspoons of garlic powder, ½ teaspoon of sea salt, ½ teaspoon of cayenne pepper, and ½ teaspoon of paprika.

2. Dredge the steak in the flour mixture, dip into the egg wash, and dredge in the bread crumb mixture. Reserve the flour mixture.

3. Place the skillet over medium-high heat and cover the bottom with peanut oil. Heat the oil to 350°F.

4. Add one of the steaks and fry for 4 minutes per side, sprinkling with sea salt and transferring to a plate in the warm oven when done. Repeat with the remaining three steaks.

5. Drain off all but 1 tablespoon of oil from the skillet. Whisk 3 tablespoons of reserved dredging flour mixture into the skillet.

6. Whisk in the chicken broth, whisking rapidly as it comes to a boil.

7. Whisk in the cream and rosemary. Continue whisking and reduce the heat to low. Simmer for 3 to 5 minutes until thick. Stir in the black pepper and season with sea salt as needed.

8. Serve the steak smothered with the gravy.

VARIATION TIP: You can adapt this recipe to the classic (if somewhat puzzling) "Chicken Fried Chicken" by replacing the cubed steaks with skinless, boneless chicken breasts.

SPICY SKILLET CHILI WITH JALAPEÑO CORN BREAD TOP

On the years when he doesn't make Cauldron Brunswick Stew (page 138) in 40-quart batches, my father makes a big batch of chili, so my sisters and I recall events based on whether it was a chili year or a Brunswick stew year. Not having six kids of my own or a chest freezer for storing massive amounts of chili, I tend to make mine one skillet at a time. This chili has the opportunity to simmer for 3 hours, which is just about the minimum amount of time needed to make chili. Anything less than that and you're just making beans.

FOR THE CHILI
1 pound 85% lean ground beef
1 tablespoon salted butter
One 28-ounce can diced tomatoes
    with the juice
2 cups water
1 onion, chopped
2 cups black beans, rinsed and drained
2 cups kidney beans,
    rinsed and drained
1 cup canned corn kernels, drained
1 tablespoon ground cumin
1 tablespoon chili powder
1 teaspoon red pepper flakes
1 teaspoon cayenne pepper
1 teaspoon ground
    chipotle chile pepper
1 teaspoon sea salt

FOR THE CORN BREAD
2 cups coarse yellow cornmeal
1 jalapeño pepper, seeded and diced
1 teaspoon sea salt
1 teaspoon baking powder
1 teaspoon baking soda
1½ cups buttermilk
1 egg
6 tablespoons (¾ stick)
    salted butter, melted
1 cup sour cream, for topping
1 cup grated Cheddar cheese,
    for topping
¼ cup diced scallions (white and
    light green parts), for topping

1. In the skillet over medium heat, brown the beef in the butter for 7 to 10 minutes, until cooked through.

2. Stir in the tomatoes, water, onion, black beans, kidney beans, corn, cumin, chili powder, red pepper flakes, cayenne pepper, chipotle chile pepper, and sea salt. Reduce the heat to low, cover, and cook for 3 hours, stirring occasionally so the chili won't stick to the bottom of the skillet.

TO MAKE THE CORN BREAD

1. Preheat the oven to 350°F.

2. In a large bowl, stir together the cornmeal, jalapeño pepper, sea salt, baking powder, and baking soda.

3. In a medium bowl, whisk the buttermilk, egg, and melted butter until well combined. Fold the buttermilk mixture into the cornmeal mixture until just evenly moistened.

4. Spoon the cornbread batter over the chili in the skillet. Bake in the oven for 35 minutes, until the cornbread is golden brown and the chili is bubbling.

5. Serve topped with the sour cream, Cheddar cheese, and scallions.

VARIATION TIP: Substitute goat cheese for the sour cream for a tangy complement to the spicy chili.

CHAPTER 8

DESSERT

CARAMEL SAUCE

After I graduated from college, our town threw a fall festival that I looked forward to for weeks. As the date approached, I thought of all the seasonal foods I was excited to eat—everything from Yeasted Apple Cider Donuts (page 58) to caramel apples. I was eager to celebrate the changing season by gorging on apple-related sweets. Unfortunately, this festival featured generic festival foods (funnel cake, chicken on a stick, Scotch eggs) in lieu of treats specific to the autumnal theme. My disappointment fueled the decision to make my own caramel sauce at home. Thankfully, caramel sauce, like most things I've tackled at home, turned out to be relatively straightforward with the help of my cast iron skillet. Over the years I've whipped up batches of caramel sauce to pour over grilled peaches, mix into turtle pies, and, of course, dip caramel apples into.

1 cup granulated sugar	½ cup heavy (whipping) cream
½ cup (1 stick) salted butter, cubed	2 teaspoons vanilla extract

1. In the skillet over medium heat, melt the sugar, stirring constantly with a wooden spoon. The sugar will clump and melt. Continue to stir as it turns amber brown, about 10 minutes total.

2. Add the butter to the skillet and stir until fully melted and incorporated.

3. Remove the skillet from the heat and add the cream. Stir rapidly as the cream and sugar bubble and combine. when fully combined, the caramel sauce will be smooth and light brown.

4. Stir in the vanilla and let cool.

5. Store the sauce in a lidded jar in the refrigerator for up to 1 week.

COOKING TIP: Watch out! Caramel sauce is *very* hot—it's literally molten sugar. My husband once made the mistake of dipping his finger into freshly made caramel sauce—resist the temptation!

PUMPKIN BREAD PUDDING

**SERVES 4 TO 6 / PREP TIME: 15 MINUTES / COOK TIME: 45 MINUTES
CAST IRON: 12-INCH SKILLET**

The first time I hosted my sister-in-law Megan and her family for dinner, I was so nervous I forgot to add spices to the pumpkin pie and sugar to the whipped cream. The result, as you can imagine, was an embarrassingly flavorless pie. I made up for it later that fall with pumpkin bread pudding—a dessert that pairs all the pumpkin spice flavors you crave during the autumnal equinox with thick, crusty bread. I like to leave about an inch of bread sticking up out of the pudding, creating a beautiful juxtaposition of crunchy bread and soft pudding.

2 tablespoons salted butter

1 loaf French bread, preferably a few
    days old, broken into 1-inch pieces

4 eggs

2 cups whole milk

2 cups pumpkin purée
    (not pumpkin pie filling)

¾ cup sugar

1 teaspoon ground cinnamon

1 teaspoon ground nutmeg

1 teaspoon ground ginger

1 teaspoon vanilla extract

1. Preheat the oven to 350°F.

2. Grease the skillet with the butter and evenly arrange the bread pieces in it.

3. In a large bowl, whisk the eggs, milk, pumpkin, sugar, cinnamon, nutmeg, ginger, and vanilla. Pour over the bread. Do not mix.

4. Bake for 45 minutes, remove from the oven, and cool, letting the filling set before serving.

VARIATION TIP: Instead of pumpkin, try 1 cup of semi-sweet chocolate chips with 1 cup of fresh strawberries.

FRIED APPLES

Fried apples are a staple of big Southern breakfasts, served alongside biscuits, country ham, and scrambled eggs. The name is a bit of a misnomer since they aren't actually fried; rather, these slow-cooked apples are browned in butter, brown sugar, and spices. Similar to apple pie filling in flavor and texture, they are delicious on their own or when served on top of pancakes, waffles, ice cream, or cookies.

½ cup (1 stick) salted butter
¼ cup packed brown sugar
2 tablespoons ground cinnamon
1 teaspoon ground allspice

1 teaspoon ground ginger
4 Granny Smith apples,
   skin left on,
   sliced ½ inch thick

1. In the skillet over medium-high heat, melt the butter.

2. Sprinkle in the brown sugar, cinnamon, allspice, and ginger. Stir to combine.

3. Add the apples and stir to coat with the butter mixture. Cook, uncovered, for 3 to 4 minutes.

4. Reduce the heat to low and simmer, uncovered, for 15 to 20 minutes until the apples soften.

PREPARATION TIP: Purée the apples for fried applesauce.

ROASTED CINNAMON PEARS

SERVES 4 / PREP TIME: 5 MINUTES / COOK TIME: 30 MINUTES
CAST IRON: 12-INCH SKILLET

Dan and I love to throw dinner parties; we thrive on cooking a meal to share with family and friends. The kitchen and dining rooms are the center of our home, and when our table is filled with guests, we're happy. When we host, I often find myself focusing so much on a main course that dessert becomes an afterthought, something that needs to be taken care of in a hurry but presented as though it was a carefully considered part of the meal. In these moments, my secret weapon is roasted pears—they are elegant, delectable, and incredibly easy.

4 Anjou pears, halved and cored
½ cup chopped pecans
1 tablespoon packed brown sugar

1 tablespoon ground cinnamon
1 tablespoon ground ginger
½ cup (1 stick) salted butter, cubed

1. Preheat the oven to 350°F.

2. Arrange the pears in the skillet, cut-side up.

3. Fill the cavity of each pear with 1 tablespoon of pecans and a sprinkle of brown sugar, cinnamon, and ginger.

4. Scatter the butter cubes evenly over the pears.

5. Bake, uncovered, for 30 minutes, until the pears are soft. Serve warm.

SERVING TIP: My favorite way to serve these pears is with sea salt caramel gelato. In lieu of that, a nice vanilla-bean ice cream with a drizzle of Caramel Sauce (page 158) is delightful.

SEA SALT SKILLET SNICKERDOODLE

SERVES 4 TO 6 / PREP TIME: 20 MINUTES / INACTIVE TIME: 1 HOUR
COOK TIME: 25 MINUTES
CAST IRON: 12-INCH SKILLET

For as long as I can remember, snickerdoodles have been my favorite cookie. They are essentially a sugar cookie dipped in cinnamon and sugar. In the case of a skillet cookie, which is one cookie rolled out to fit the size of your skillet, the cinnamon-sugar mixture becomes a topping.

FOR THE CINNAMON-SUGAR
¼ cup granulated sugar
1 tablespoon ground cinnamon
½ teaspoon sea salt

FOR THE COOKIE
2¾ cups all-purpose flour
1½ teaspoons cream of tartar
1 teaspoon baking soda
½ teaspoon sea salt
1 cup (2 sticks) salted butter,
    at room temperature
1½ cups granulated sugar
2 eggs
1 teaspoon vanilla extract

TO MAKE THE CINNAMON-SUGAR

In a small bowl, stir together the sugar, cinnamon, and sea salt. Set aside.

TO MAKE THE COOKIE

1. In a large bowl, whisk the flour, cream of tartar, baking soda, and sea salt.

2. In the bowl of a stand mixer, cream together the butter and granulated sugar at medium-high speed. Add the eggs, one at a time, beating to incorporate after each addition. Mix in the vanilla.

3. Reduce the mixer speed to low, and slowly add the flour mixture to the butter mixture, mixing until fully combined. Cover the dough and chill for 1 hour.

4. Preheat the oven to 375°F.

5. Press the dough into the skillet. Sprinkle the cinnamon-sugar evenly over the top.

6. Bake for 20 to 25 minutes until cooked through. Cool before cutting into wedges and serving.

BLUEBERRY MOUNTAIN PIE

SERVES 4 TO 6 / PREP TIME: 10 MINUTES / COOK TIME: 40 MINUTES
CAST IRON: DUTCH OVEN

Every year for my birthday, my grandma, Bobbie, would make me a mountain pie served hot with whole-bean vanilla ice cream. Mountain pie is somewhere between a cobbler and a sonker, a family favorite that my Great-Aunt Jinx thinks she might have picked up somewhere in Tennessee. The beauty lies in its simplicity—cake batter poured into hot melted butter, and topped with blueberries. The cake rises up, enveloping the blueberries, butter bubbling all around. There is one cardinal rule when it comes to mountain pie: Do not mix the ingredients once they're in the Dutch oven. Trust me.

½ cup (1 stick) salted butter

1 cup all-purpose flour

½ cup sugar

1¼ teaspoons baking powder

1 teaspoon sea salt

¾ cup whole milk

1 teaspoon vanilla extract

3 cups blueberries

1. Preheat the oven to 350°F.

2. Add the butter to the Dutch oven, and place it, uncovered, in the warming oven to melt.

3. In a medium bowl, mix the flour, sugar, baking powder, sea salt, milk, and vanilla until combined. Pour the batter over the melted butter. Do not mix!

4. Sprinkle the top with the blueberries. Do not mix!

5. Bake for 40 minutes until bubbling and cooked through.

VARIATION TIP: Substitute strawberries, blackberries, peaches, or cherries (or almost any other fruit that strikes your fancy) for the blueberries. You might even want to try Fried Apples (page 160)!

CAYENNE CANDIED PECANS

MAKES 1 CUP / PREP TIME: 15 MINUTES / COOK TIME: 20 MINUTES
CAST IRON: 10-INCH SKILLET

Candied pecans are one of those treats I like to keep on hand for snacking, sprinkling on salads, or mixing into ice cream. Making them is relatively easy, and they have a wonderfully long shelf life. Adding a bit of cayenne pepper to the spice blend provides a surprising kick in an otherwise sweet and crunchy treat.

2 egg whites
1 teaspoon vanilla extract
1 cup whole pecans
¼ cup granulated sugar

1 tablespoon cayenne pepper
1 tablespoon ground cinnamon
½ teaspoon ground nutmeg
¼ cup packed brown sugar

1. Preheat the oven to 350°F.

2. In a medium bowl, whisk the egg whites until frothy. Whisk in the vanilla.

3. Add the pecans and stir to coat completely.

4. In a small bowl, stir together the granulated sugar, cayenne pepper, cinnamon, and nutmeg. Transfer half to a second small bowl and set aside.

5. Mix the brown sugar into one of the bowls of spiced sugar mixture. Coat the pecans evenly in the brown sugar-spiced sugar blend. Transfer them to the skillet.

6. Bake for 10 minutes, stir well, and bake for 10 minutes more.

7. Remove the pecans from the oven and add the reserved spiced sugar. Stir well to coat, and let cool completely before serving.

VARIATION TIP: Experiment with different spice blends, perhaps substituting ground cardamom for cayenne pepper.

PEANUT BUTTER BROWNIE

SERVES 4 TO 6 / PREP TIME: 20 MINUTES / COOK TIME: 30 MINUTES
CAST IRON: 10-INCH SKILLET

A classic brownie recipe is an important part of every cook's repertoire, and a base recipe opens up the opportunity for endless variations. Dan's particular favorite is a chocolate peanut butter brownie, where the brownie batter is divided in half and a generous layer of peanut butter is spread between the layers. We find they are best served fresh out of the oven with a generous spoonful of peanut butter gelato.

½ cup (1 stick) salted butter,
   at room temperature
1 cup packed brown sugar
4 eggs, lightly beaten
1 teaspoon vanilla extract

¼ cup buttermilk
1½ cups unsweetened cocoa powder
⅔ cup all-purpose flour
¼ teaspoon baking soda
1 cup peanut butter

1. Preheat the oven to 350°F.

2. In a medium bowl, stir together the butter, brown sugar, eggs, and vanilla.

3. Stir in the buttermilk.

4. In a another bowl, gently whisk together the cocoa powder, flour, and baking soda. Fold the flour mixture into the butter mixture.

5. Spoon half of the batter into the skillet and spread it out evenly. Top with the peanut butter and spread it evenly. Then pour the remaining batter, spreading it in an even layer.

6. Bake for 25 to 30 minutes, until cooked through. Allow to cool slightly before serving.

VARIATION TIP: Instead of peanut butter, mix 1 cup of chocolate chunks into the batter for double chocolate brownies.

MIXED BERRY COBBLER

SERVES 6 TO 8 / PREP TIME: 15 MINUTES / COOK TIME: 35 MINUTES
CAST IRON: 12-INCH SKILLET

In the spring and summer, when the markets are bursting with berries, I cannot resist loading up my basket. I'll bring home buckets of strawberries from a local farm, stop to pick mulberries in the park down the street, and raid the blueberry bushes by the neighborhood creek. Once I've eaten my fill of fresh berries, I start to work them into jams, jellies, preserves, ice creams and, best of all, cobblers. There's something delightfully straightforward about a cobbler—mixed fruit topped with a crust, spices, butter, and brown sugar—making it the ideal dessert for long summer nights.

FOR THE LATTICE-TOP DOUGH
1¼ cup all-purpose flour
½ cup (1 stick) salted butter, melted
1 tablespoon sugar
Pinch sea salt
¼ cup cold water

FOR THE FILLING
6 cups mixed fresh (or frozen) strawberries, blueberries, and blackberries
1½ tablespoons salted butter
1 teaspoon vanilla extract

Preheat the oven to 350°F.

TO MAKE THE DOUGH

In a large bowl, combine the flour, butter, sugar, and sea salt in a food processor. Pulse until the texture resembles cornmeal. While pulsing, add water, 1 tablespoon at a time, until it forms a dough ball. Wrap with plastic wrap and chill in the refrigerator for at least one hour.

TO MAKE THE FILLING

1. Slice the strawberries. Clean the blueberries and blackberries.

2. In the skillet over medium heat, melt the butter.

3. Add the vanilla, strawberries, blueberries, and blackberries. Cook for 3 to 5 minutes (if using fresh berries) or 10 to 12 minutes (if using frozen berries). Remove from heat and set aside.

1. Remove the chilled dough from the refrigerator and on a lightly-floured surface or baking mat, roll it into a circle that's about 3 inches larger than the diameter of the skillet.

2. Using a knife or pizza wheel, cut the dough into 1-inch strips.

3. On top of the berries in the skillet, place the dough strips in one direction with about a 1-inch gap between strips.

4. Beginning in the middle and going outward, weave the remaining strips in the opposite direction. Trim the ends of the dough so that they're flush with the skillet edge.

5. Bake for 30 to 35 minutes. Let cool before serving.

SERVING TIP: Serve hot with vanilla ice cream.

APPLE & GOUDA SKILLET PIES

SERVES 7 / PREP TIME: 30 MINUTES / INACTIVE TIME: 1 HOUR
COOK TIME: 40 MINUTES
CAST IRON: 12-INCH SKILLET AND BISCUIT PAN

One of the most underrated TV shows of my generation is *Pushing Daisies*. Not only is it a fantastic and quirky crime drama (my genre of choice), but the whole show centers around a pie shop. And since pie is my dessert of choice, that fact endeared me to the show immediately. In fact, it was an episode of *Pushing Daisies* that taught me the beauty of adding cheese to a sweet pie, something I will always appreciate. While I've had great success with pear and Gruyère (delicious and rhyming to boot), my favorite combination is apple and Gouda. Mixing the Gouda directly into the crust adds wonderful flavor and helps hold the crust together, while the smokiness of the cheese is lovely with the apple and cinnamon in the filling.

FOR THE DOUGH
2½ cups all-purpose flour
1 cup cubed smoked Gouda cheese
¾ cup (1½ sticks) salted butter, cubed
3 tablespoons granulated sugar
¼ teaspoon sea salt
¼ cup water
2 tablespoons salted butter
1 egg, beaten

FOR THE FILLING
4 tablespoons (½ stick) salted butter
6 Honey Crisp or Pink Lady apples,
    skin left on, cored and sliced
    ½ inch thick
4 tablespoons packed
    light brown sugar
1 teaspoon ground cinnamon
1 teaspoon ground ginger
1 teaspoon vanilla extract

TO MAKE THE DOUGH

1. In a food processor (or blender), combine the flour, Gouda cheese, butter, granulated sugar, and sea salt. Pulse until the mixture is crumbled and roughly resembles coarse cornmeal.

2. While pulsing, add the water, 1 tablespoon at a time, until it forms a ball. Wrap the dough in plastic wrap and chill for 1 hour.

TO MAKE THE FILLING

1. Preheat the oven to 350°F.

2. In the skillet over medium heat, melt 2 tablespoons of butter.

3. Stir the apples into the melted butter.

4. Add the brown sugar, cinnamon, ginger, and vanilla. Cook for 15 minutes, stirring frequently.

5. With the remaining 2 tablespoons of butter, grease the wells of the biscuit pan.

6. Divide the dough into two portions, one slightly larger than the other. Divide the larger portion into 7 chunks and leave the smaller portion whole. On a floured work surface (or a silicone baking mat), start with the larger portion of dough, and roll out each chunk of piecrust into a 5-inch circle about ¼ inch thick. Press 1 circle into each well of the biscuit pan. Fill each well with the apples.

7. Roll out the remaining smaller portion of the dough flat and about ¼ inch thick. With a 4-inch circular piecrust cutter, cut out 7 rounds. Top each pie with a lid, crimping the bottom crust to the top crust and pinching off any excess. Cut 3 or 4 1-inch slits into each pie top.

8. Brush the top of each pie with some of the beaten egg. Place the biscuit pan into a baking pan.

9. Bake for 35 to 40 minutes, until browned and bubbling.

10. Let cool for 5 to 10 minutes before gently removing the pies from the pan. Serve warm.

VARIATION TIP: Try a pear and Gruyère cheese pie by substituting pears for the apples and Gruyère for the Gouda.

TAR HEEL PIE

SERVES 6 TO 8 / PREP TIME: 25 MINUTES / INACTIVE TIME: 1 HOUR
COOK TIME: 40 MINUTES
CAST IRON: 10-INCH SKILLET

One of my grandmother's go-to recipes for special occasions was a chocolate chess pie, a category of Southern pie that's basically made of egg, flour, and butter. Chess pies come in many varieties, from lemon to vinegar, though my favorite is the chocolate chess. It's smooth, rich, and deeply chocolaty. With the addition of chopped pecans, it becomes Tar Heel pie, so named for the Tar Heel State (North Carolina). Both chocolate chess pie and Tar Heel pie lend themselves nicely to a skillet, the deep-dish pie taking on a brownie-like quality. As my grandma always said, it's best to indulge in just a sliver.

FOR THE DOUGH
1¼ cups all-purpose flour
½ cup (1 stick) salted butter
1 tablespoon granulated sugar
Pinch sea salt
¼ cup cold water

FOR THE FILLING
½ cup (1 stick) salted butter, melted, still hot
1 cup semi-sweet chocolate chips
2 eggs
1¼ cups chopped pecans, divided
1 cup plus 2 tablespoons packed dark brown sugar, divided
½ cup all-purpose flour
1 teaspoon vanilla extract

TO MAKE THE DOUGH

1. In a food processor (or blender), combine the flour, butter, granulated sugar, and sea salt. Pulse until the mixture is crumbled and roughly resembles coarse cornmeal.

2. While pulsing, add the water 1 tablespoon at a time until it forms a ball. Wrap the ball in plastic wrap and chill for 1 hour.

1. Preheat the oven to 350°F.

2. In a medium bowl, stir together the hot butter and chocolate chips until the chocolate melts completely.

3. In another medium bowl, whisk the eggs.

4. Stir in 1 cup of pecans, 1 cup of brown sugar, and the flour and vanilla. Fold this mixture into the chocolate.

5. Press the dough into the bottom and up the sides of the skillet.

6. Pour the batter into the skillet on top of the dough.

7. Sprinkle the remaining ¼ cup of pecans and the remaining 2 tablespoons of brown sugar over the top.

8. Bake for 30 to 40 minutes. The pie can be slightly soft in the middle, but should be firmly set around the edges.

9. Let cool and set completely before cutting into narrow wedges and serving.

VARIATION TIP: Make the classic variation of this pie, the Chocolate Chess Pie, by simply omitting the pecans.

BOURBON PEACH PIE

SERVES 6 TO 8 / PREP TIME: 25 MINUTES / INACTIVE TIME: 1 HOUR
COOK TIME: 35 MINUTES
CAST IRON: 12-INCH SKILLET

Nothing is more heavenly than a ripe peach. This recipe, for a classic peach pie with a bourbon twist, is always on the menu during peach season. The spicy flavor of the bourbon plays against the sweet, tart flavor of the peaches, pairing so nicely that this summer I might just try my hand at a peach and bourbon cocktail to pour alongside my pie.

FOR THE DOUGH
2½ cups all-purpose flour,
　　plus more for dusting
¾ cup (1½ sticks) cold
　　salted butter, cubed
3 tablespoons granulated sugar
¼ teaspoon sea salt
¼ cup cold water
1 egg, beaten

FOR THE FILLING
7 peaches, peeled, pitted,
　　and sliced ½ inch thick
¼ cup all-purpose flour
3 tablespoons packed brown sugar
2 tablespoons bourbon
1 teaspoon vanilla extract

TO MAKE THE DOUGH

1.　In a food processor (or blender), add the flour, butter, granulated sugar, and sea salt. Pulse until the mixture is crumbled and roughly resembles coarse cornmeal.

2.　While pulsing, add the water 1 tablespoon at a time until it forms a ball. Wrap the ball in plastic wrap and chill for 1 hour.

1. Preheat the oven to 375°F.

2. In a large bowl, toss together the peaches, flour, brown sugar, bourbon, and vanilla.

3. On a floured work surface (or a silicone baking mat), roll out half the dough into a 12-inch circle about ¼ inch thick. Press into the bottom of the skillet. Top with the peaches.

4. Roll out the remaining dough into another 12-inch circle about ¼ inch thick. Cut it into 1-inch strips. Arrange the strips into a lattice formation (see Preparation Tip) on top of the peaches.

5. With a pastry brush, brush the beaten egg evenly over the dough.

6. Bake for 30 to 35 minutes. Let cool slightly to set before serving warm.

PREPARATION TIP: To make a lattice top crust, lay down half of the dough strips in one direction. Starting in the middle, weave in the remaining strips in opposite crosswise direction. Note that thicker strips are easier to work with if you're just learning this technique. Alternatively, just lay the second 12-inch dough circle over the peaches, crimp the edges, and cut slits into the top to release steam.

BAKING TIP: For juicy pies, place the pie dish on the middle oven rack, and put a sheet of foil on the rack below it to catch any drips.

ANCESTRAL LEMON CHESS PIE

MAKES 7 / PREP TIME: 25 MINUTES / INACTIVE TIME: 1 HOUR
COOK TIME: 30 MINUTES
CAST IRON: BISCUIT PAN

I recently attended a conference at the University of North Carolina on the history of the state's foodways. One of the biggest takeaways came during a talk about early colonial food. The speaker, Kay Moss, explained that over the course of the past 300 years, the amount of butter and egg in a chess pie has remained consistent, but the amount of sugar has tripled as it became more widely available and less of a luxury item. Almost immediately upon returning home, I tried my hand at an ancestral lemon chess pie, more like those on a colonial table than on my grandmother's. The results were incredible. By reducing the amount of sugar, the lemon juice is dominant, making the flavor tart, with a creamy texture akin to custard. When it comes to chess pies, I'll be taking a page from the eighteenth-century cooks from now on.

FOR THE DOUGH
2 cups all-purpose flour,
    plus more for dusting
½ cup (1 stick) cold
    salted butter, cubed
1 tablespoon sugar
Pinch sea salt
⅓ cup cold water

FOR THE FILLING
½ cup (1 stick) salted butter,
    melted, plus 1 tablespoon
¼ cup sugar
4 eggs
Juice of 4 lemons
1 teaspoon vanilla extract
Pinch sea salt

TO MAKE THE DOUGH

In a food processor (or blender), add the flour, the cold butter cubes, sugar, and sea salt. Pulse until the butter is fully cut into the flour and the texture resembles coarse cornmeal. While pulsing, slowly add the water, 1 tablespoon at a time, until it forms a ball. Cover the ball in plastic wrap and chill for 1 hour.

1. In a medium bowl, stir together the melted butter and sugar.

2. Add the eggs, one at a time, mixing after each addition.

3. Stir in the lemon juice and vanilla.

4. Preheat the oven to 375°F.

5. On a floured work surface (or a silicone baking mat), roll out the dough to ¼ inch thick. With a 4-inch pastry cutter, cut 7 dough rounds.

6. With the remaining 1 tablespoon of butter, grease the wells of the biscuit pan.

7. Press the dough rounds into the wells of the pan.

8. Fill each well almost to the top with filling.

9. Bake for 25 to 30 minutes, or until the filling is firm and the crust edges begin to brown.

10. Let cool slightly before serving.

SERVING TIP: Serve topped with fresh figs and a drizzle of honey.

MEASUREMENT CONVERSIONS

VOLUME EQUIVALENTS (DRY)

US Standard	Metric (approximate)
⅛ teaspoon	0.5 mL
¼ teaspoon	1 mL
½ teaspoon	2 mL
¾ teaspoon	4 mL
1 teaspoon	5 mL
1 tablespoon	15 mL
¼ cup	59 mL
⅓ cup	79 mL
½ cup	118 mL
⅔ cup	156 mL
¾ cup	177 mL
1 cup	235 mL
2 cups or 1 pint	475 mL
3 cups	700 mL
4 cups or 1 quart	1 L
½ gallon	2 L
1 gallon	4 L

VOLUME EQUIVALENTS (LIQUID)

US Standard	US Standard (ounces)	Metric (approximate)
2 tablespoons	1 fl. oz.	30 mL
¼ cup	2 fl. oz.	60 mL
½ cup	4 fl. oz.	120 mL
1 cup	8 fl. oz.	240 mL
1½ cups	12 fl. oz.	355 mL
2 cups or 1 pint	16 fl. oz.	475 mL
4 cups or 1 quart	32 fl. oz.	1 L
1 gallon	128 fl. oz.	4 L

OVEN TEMPERATURES

Fahrenheit (F)	Celsius (C) (approximate)
250°F	120°C
300°F	150°C
325°F	165°C
350°F	180°C
375°F	190°C
400°F	200°C
425°F	220°C
450°F	230°C

RESOURCES

Much of what I know about cast iron has come from years of cooking and working with it. When it came to studying the history of cast iron, I found these sources to be invaluable:

The Book of Griswold and Wagner: Favorite Wapak, Sidney Holloware by David G. Smith and Chuck Wafford

The Book of Wagner & Griswold: Martin, Lodge, Vollrath, Excelsior by David G. Smith

The Cast Iron Collector: www.castironcollector.com

RECIPE INDEX

INDEX

ACKNOWLEDGMENTS

Thank you to my father, Ken, for teaching me that cast iron is something to be treasured and treated with care. Thank you for sharing your love of cooking with me, and for always encouraging me to follow my interests and passions.

Thank you to my friends and family for helping me test recipes and for giving constructive criticism. I could not have finished this book without the carefully considered feedback and suggestions from you. Special thanks to the heavy lifters, Lauren Jones, Liz Flint-Somerville, Heather Calkins, Mary Regan, and Aaron Clark. Lauren, Bradley, and Genevieve—thank you for letting me hover obnoxiously in the kitchen door, watching as you tried to interpret and cook my recipes.

Thank you to Liz Flint-Somerville for taking the time to painstakingly read the book and share your notes, feedback, and thoughts. This book is better because of your careful blue pen.

Thank you to Lauren Jones not only for testing a large chunk of the recipes but also for watching my child so I could work on the book. I could not have written this without your help.

Thank you to Meg Ilasco and the team at Callisto for giving me the opportunity to write a book I've always wanted to write, and bearing with me as I learned how to be a working mom.

Thank you, most of all, to my husband, Dan. Thank you for encouraging me to take on a big project while our son was still a newborn; thank you for offering coffee, wine, and encouragement when I wasn't sure I could meet deadlines; thank you for taking baby duty so I could sneak away to write; and thank you, most of all, for reminding me I am able. Also, thanks for always standing by with a fire extinguisher when I get to the "light it on fire" step of cast iron restoration.

ABOUT THE AUTHOR

ELENA ROSEMOND-HOERR was born and raised in Durham, North Carolina. Through her father's side of the family, her roots in North Carolina's foothills and mountains reach back to the early colonies, and she has the heirloom cast iron to prove it. In 2008 she created the Southern food blog *Biscuits and Such* (Biscuitsandsuch.com), which started her down a path that would include writing cookbooks and magazine features, and an unexpected career studying and contributing to Southern food culture. She currently resides in coastal North Carolina with her husband, Dan, their son, Everett, and their two misfit dogs.